A US FEMINIST IN SAUDI ARABIA 1980-1982

MARGARET DRAKE

iUniverse, Inc.
New York   Bloomington

A US Feminist in Saudi Arabia: 1980-1982

iUniverse books may be ordered through booksellers or by contacting:

iUniverse
1663 Liberty Drive
Bloomington, IN 47403
www.iuniverse.com
1-800-Authors (1-800-288-4677)

Because of the dynamic nature of the Internet, any Web addresses or links contained in this book may have changed since publication and may no longer be valid. The views expressed in this work are solely those of the author and do not necessarily reflect the views of the publisher, and the publisher hereby disclaims any responsibility for them.

ISBN: 978-1-4502-2482-6 (sc)
ISBN: 978-1-4502-2483-3 (ebook)

Printed in the United States of America

iUniverse rev. date: 05/11/2010

Table of Contents

PREFACE

This manuscript was originally written during July and August 1982, immediately after I returned from the two years in Riyadh, Saudi Arabia. At that time, it was a sort of catharsis for pent up feelings from living in a repressive society. It was another seven years before I got a personal computer. And another eighteen years after that before I decided it was time to type it into my word processing program. The backward view of twenty-eight to thirty years did cause me to make some revisions as I went along; however the main text is as I wrote it in the summer of 1982. In those long ago times, footnotes were still often at the bottom of the page. In this version, footnotes are incorporated into explanations in the text. The feelings expressed at that time have not been changed in the text, though they sometimes appear different to me now from the backward look of age and further overseas experience.

Two things happened just before I left Saudi in 1982 that I was reluctant to write about at that time as they were unresolved and I did not want to endanger my own position or my friend's safety. The first thing was that I was cheated out of approximately $8000 over the two years I was working there. I was hired at a salary that was approximately the same as the one I made in California but I was going for adventure, not for the money. It was about $4000 more than other employees at my level from the Middle East made. At the end of the first year, they told all western faculty members that they were taking off all the recruitment increments that they had offered in order to get us to come and then they were raising everybody's salary 20% so the Middle Easterners salaries would be equivalent with Westerners. This ended up giving me the same salary both years though I had been promised substantial raises during my interview. The other $4000 they cheated me out of was that I discovered that, along with the physical therapist and laboratory technicians, I fell into a "hard to recruit" category of jobs for which they were supposed to pay us 25% more than our base salary. The physical therapist and I together started at the lowest level of the hierarchy of the University administrators and worked ourselves up finally to the Chancellor asking for this "hard to recruit" supplement. I went to see him alone just five days before I was to leave the Kingdom. He promised that I would get the money eventually but since my visa expired in five days, someone else would have to pick up the money and send it to me. I got all the paper work done so my friend could receive my money. She went to the payroll office with the papers and they would never give her the money. I thought of all kinds of schemes to try to get the money but after a visit to a lawyer, I came to the realization it would cost me too much to seek further for what I was owed by the Saudi government.

The second incident was when a friend I had made there asked me to be her chaperon while she went to a western hotel to meet a man who was a possible suitor. I went with her on three occasions to different hotels or venues for her to try to assess this man's possibilities. I did not write this in the original manuscript because she had not married him and indeed later broke it off. I was not a proper chaperon by Saudi standards though the hotels accepted me in that position. She might have had severe repercussions from her family had it become know, thus I did not write it at that time. I wanted to protect her. She has long since married someone else.

I added Chapter 15, the Epilogue, in order to incorporate the more recent news and information about the Kingdom of Saudi Arabia. If a reader is interested in finding out more about the lives of modern Saudi women, the novel *Girls of Riyadh* by Rajaa Alsanea (2005) shows that the restrictions on females have changed little from my time there thirty years ago.

When I wrote the book in 1982, I had been a resident of California for more than twenty years in two different periods. Consequently, I titled the book *A California Woman Sees behind the Veil*. However, I have not been a resident of California since 1983; it no longer seemed the appropriate title for the book. I asked a number of my female friends and relatives for suggestions. Some of them were:

Seeing beyond the Veil
Wahabi Woman
Behind the Veil, Saudi Arabia 1980-1982
Looking Beyond the Veil, Saudi Arabia 1980-1982
Feminist among the Wahabis, an OT Perspective
The Wahine and the Wahabis
A Feminist in Saudi Arabia

An American Feminist in Saudi Arabia (1980-1982)
The Shrouded Feminist: Behind the Veil in Saudi Arabia
Veiled: A Western Woman's View of Saudi Arabia
Saudi Arabia: A Western Woman's First Hand Experience
Behind the Veil: A Western Woman's Experience
An American Occupational Therapist Teaching Nursing in Saudi Arabia in
*   1980-1982.*

Four of the women all mentioned *A Feminist in Saudi Arabia*. This helped me choose this title.

ACKNOWLEDGEMENTS

There are probably many people whom I have forgotten in the last twenty eight years since I wrote this book. I ask their forgiveness for not remembering all their names. But I do especially want to mention my boss, Jackie Tiller RN and a colleague, Mary Hipp RN. I was probably closer to these two women than to any others during my time in Saudi Arabia. For helping me with the title I want to thank my sister Ann Wagner, her daughter Muriel Hoover, my niece Bonnie Goodell, my cousin Barbara Murray, my friends Susan Haik, Joanne Bienvenu, Patty Barnett, Janet Tillman and Joanna Fitzgerald. Also I want to thank Tom Young for help with my faded old photographs.

1

HOW IT HAPPENED

Here's how it happened - - my two years in the repressive and puritanical 20th century nation, Saudi Arabia; me, a feminist, whose adulthood was reached during the "hippy" sixties, tangled with Islam in Saudi Arabia. Saudi Arabia had its start in 1902, thus existing as a governmental entity only during the 20th and into the 21st century. Many people call it the "a 20th century nation going on the 14th" because the Arabic calendar dates from the year 622, when the Prophet Mohamed fled to Mecca so 1982 became 1402 in the Hijera (date of migration) Islamic calendar. However, others took this phase to mean they were entering the 14th century in regard to their mores.

I had been divorced from my first husband for fifteen years and my second husband for eleven years. With no children to hold me down and require attention, I had been able to devote my full attention to dating, men, love affairs, between bouts of sex education and incidentally, other education as well. I had completed a second bachelor's degree and a master degree between and during the affairs and work.

Saudi Arabia, on the other hand, seemed to have as its main objective suppression of sexual expression, art expression which was important to me as my masters was in art therapy and suppressions of female independence. These features of the Saudi culture are in direct contrast to the emphasis and development of the American culture during the "hippy" era, my era.

For two years, ever since I had spent a month in Britain in 1978, I had toyed with the fantasy of working my way around the world or doing the more conservative thing, which turned out to be the more daring, getting a job in another country. Since the age of eighteen when I had been majoring

1

in languages in junior college, I had wanted to be employed in that most romantic of all settings – OVERSEAS! In those days, I had had fantasies of Rio de Janeiro or Buenos Aires, never any place as "weird" and "foreign" as the MIDDLE EAST! Old movies like *Casablanca* or *Lawrence of Arabia* were my last resort in TV watching.

When my work cycle came around on the one and one half year mark and I began to itch for a different job again, there were only two countries advertising for my skills, Japan and Saudi Arabia. There is a normal "burnout cycle" in the helping professions that I had been unwittingly experiencing. Every eighteen months, I felt a strong urge to change.

"Is burnout inevitable? Some professionals think so and assume that it is only a matter of time before they will burn out and have to change jobs. The period of time most often cited in one psychiatric ward was 1½ years; in free clinics it was usually one year and some poverty lawyers spoke of reduction of a former four year stint down to two" (Maslach, 1976).

I sent my resume' off with excitement over the prospects. Each new advertisement engendered new fantasies and excitement. I had first seen the advertisement for the University of Riyadh on July 12, 1980. I knew Saudi Arabia was a peninsula between Africa and India in the Middle East, but nothing more. I immediately went to the public library and found two shelves of books on Saudi Arabia. My first choice was At *the Drop of a Veil* by Marianne Alireza (1971), the only one with a female author. I needed to know from a woman and she told me, though her story was thirty five years old. In spite of her tale of loss of freedoms, I sent my résumé. Then I promptly forgot it and got on to reading more advertisements and sending off more résumés. When I received the first telegram from the Consulate of Saudi Arabia in Houston Texas, I was surprised and elated. They requested me to call "collect" to make an appointment for an interview. So I did. They asked me to come to Riyadh to teach in the University. So I did.

Between my interview on July 29th and my date of departure on August 24th, I wrote off to my seven alma-maters to ask them to send my official transcripts to the University of Riyadh. During my eventual stay there, the celebration of the 25th anniversary of its founding was held. The university changed its name from the University of Riyadh, back to the original name King Saud University. King Saud was the second ruler of this monarchy. He was deposed in favor of his brother Faisal in October 1964.

I got each of my last four employers to write a notarized letter verifying employment. Believe me, that meant driving all over Los Angeles County. Then I had to go to the county clerk's office in two counties to have the notary's seals verified. This then had to be sent to the STATE Secretary of State for verification of the county clerks' seals before the final validation of the

California Secretary of State seal by the Department of State in Washington D.C. so they could be sent on to the University. This was done just to prove I had done what I had said I had done. For some reason I avoided wondering why they were so distrustful.

They also required the original copies of all my higher education diplomas. Four years before, when I received my master degree on heavy creamy parchment, I had proudly decoupaged all my validating papers (i.e. AA, BA, BS, MA, OTR, and ATR) and displayed them in my bedroom. "Pride always gets punished", my mother used to tell me. And she was right! Now I would be required to carry these darned pieces of wood halfway around the world.

One does not change one's preoccupations easily, so in spite of my growing awareness, from my reading, of the sexual repression I was to face, I automatically began to think about how I could continue my same sexual behavior patterns: specifically, I wondered how I could carry my diaphragm in through Saudi customs despite my knowledge that birth-control was forbidden with severe punishments of jail and lashes for offenders of their sexual laws. At church on a Sunday shortly before I was to leave, I met an old friend who was close to seventy years, a woman from my first "women's consciousness raising" group. I reported to her that I had finally solved this problem. Simple! I would wear my diaphragm in. She looked at me thoughtfully and said, "I always wondered why those travelers to Mexico and Turkey and countries where drug punishments are severe, persist in taking marijuana in with them." After only a moment of thought, I made a decision and responded to her. "You are right. I won't take the diaphragm. I can do without it for a year." So I did.

The last week was a nightmare of packing personal belongings, renting my house, storing my car, arranging business matters, shipping my sewing machine, autoharp and typewriter, say goodbye to my friends and my community. I was emotionally preparing myself to do without the solace of my loved ones for at least ten months. Every day of the last week, I called the consulate in Houston to check on where my passport and visa were. Each day they said they had been sent. But it had not arrived by the day I was to leave. I began to wonder with whom I was dealing. So I called again. They assured me it was on its way by overnight messenger service. They also arranged for the flight the following day. And indeed, the next morning, the passport arrived properly stamped with my visa. I locked my house to await my new tenants. Off to the airport!

When the airplane was over the Rockies and I temporarily relaxed, I began to write to a close woman friend. The impact of my situation came strongly into focus. The flood gates opened and I wept to realize I would be without friends' support, chiding and understanding, except by letter.

3

Airplane weepers are fairly common apparently since no one paid me any mind.

When the plane took off from De Gaulle Airport in Paris, they announced that we would make two stops before Riyadh, first in Rome and then in Jeddah. After Paris, I didn't have any more intoxicating drinks as I was now on SAUDIA AIRLINES, where in accordance with Islamic law, no liquor or wine was allowed. But they did serve bottled Mecca water which duly impressed me. My initiation into the mysteries of Islam had begun, because what this water was supposed to do me still remained a mystery. At that time while drinking it, I wondered if it were for external or internal use. I felt sure I was not supposed to cross myself with it. Eventually, I found the fine print that told me it was for ingestion. I knew that Mecca was forbidden to me, but was unaware of whether Mecca water was also forbidden to me. Since the steward and stewardesses looked Middle Eastern, I figured they would not allow me to defile anything, so I drank it.

During my last week before I left, one of the questions I had asked the Saudi Consulate on the phone was whether I could buy vitamins in Riyadh. They had assured me that I could. Never-the-less, I knew from previous moves that even in California, it is sometimes hard to find all the amenities such as a post office, craft supply store or a health-food store in a town new to me. So I had purchased enough of my favorite vitamins to last at least three months. I figured that that would allow me time to find the vitamin source in Riyadh before running out. By the time I had packed these new sealed bottles, I still had a half empty bottle of Vitamin C. Firstly, I felt I had better carry it with me on the flight since all the new research said a person could use up to 1000 International Units of Vitamin C in an hour under stressful conditions. I figured that going to Saudi Arabia for a year could be considered a stressful condition, so I planned to use up the bottle enroute. Secondly, all our fables about the Middle East tell of the harsh punishments for foreigners suspected of carrying drugs. This was reinforced in the movie "Midnight Express". They might think that my open bottle of Vitamin C was a way of smuggling drugs. So I planned to take all of it before landing and then hide the empty bottle in the rubbish bin in the airplane toilet. But they surprised me by announcing that we were landing in Jeddah and we were taxiing into the terminal where we would deplane and go through "hand luggage" customs. And here I was with this incriminating ¼ full bottle of Vitamin C in my handbag. So I thrust it into the pocket in the seat in front of me, figuring to retrieve it upon reboarding since the stewardess assured me that we would be on the same plane to Riyadh.

In the terminal, after a cursory search of my handbag and my bag of decoupaged wood, I, with other continuing passengers stood for one and one half hours waiting to reboard. All this time I was nervous for fear that the cabin attendants had found my little cache of Vitamin C and knowing my seat number by the computer would have notified the proper drug authorities who would come and cart me off to prison before enplaning. Little did I know that they are never that organized!

While in the airport, my nervousness caused me to need the ladies lounge. When I entered a partitioned off area, I had my first experience of seeing women entirely covered in black. As I rounded the moveable screen at the edge of the segregated women's waiting area, I saw a row of the faceless black figures squatting on the floor with their backs to screen. Gradually, as the shock effect of this row of hidden humans wore off, I realized that several were holding sleeping children within the folds of their black cloth. I said to myself, "You'll get used to it." Little did I know, that I would never get used to it, that each new experience when I was unprepared for it mentally, of seeing numbers of faceless black figures, shocked me again.

When reboard was announced, I aimed to find my Vitamin C bottle, but as I attempted to go toward the rear down the aisle to my former seat, the stewardess informed me that I was to go forward into the family section. I informed her that I was alone, not part of a family. "Never mind," she said, "Sit with the families." This was my first experience with knowing that since I was a woman, I was assumed to be part of somebody's family. No more of this "Woman alone!" I must belong to somebody!

Not wanting to make a scene, I complied. During the one remaining hour flight, I expected momentarily that the male who now occupied my seat would find my Vitamin C bottle and honorably turn it into the stewardess who would, FBI fashion, find me and turn me in to the police at Riyadh and maybe even place me under arrest on the airplane. But nobody seemed to be observing me except faceless women in the "Family Section." Jet lag and sleeplessness do strange things to the traveler's mind!

I landed in Riyadh twenty five and a half hours after boarding the airplane in Los Angeles. Four white robed men met me, swept me through customs, bypassing passport control, health inspection and waiting mobs, depositing me into a car to be taken to me new home in Riyadh.

REFERENCES:

Alireza, Marianne (1971) *At the Drop of a Veil*. NY: Houghton Mifflin.

Maslach, Christina (1976). Burned out. *Department of Health and Human Services Quarterly*, Vol. 34:

2

WATER & BEVERAGE

The plethora of new stimuli to which I was then exposed required organization for the information to be assimilable. From a fifteen year history of association with the "humanistic psychology" movement, I was able to use Abraham Maslow's (1968) *hierarchy of human needs* to organize my thoughts. It is one way of 'putting first things first'. He prioritized these needs accordingly; <u>first</u>, physiological (i.e. water, food, clothes, shelter and sex) <u>second</u>, safety (i.e. health care, government) <u>third</u>, belonging and love (i.e. families, friends, and affection) <u>fourth</u>, esteem and recognition (i.e. status and work) <u>fifth</u> self-actualization and aesthetics (i.e. art, order, religion and spiritual goals). I have used his hierarchy as an outline upon which to base my own hierarchy of needs. Consequently, there was some slight deviations from the order into which Maslow ranked things. Further I was unable to separate the social experience of being a woman from the physiological aspects of sex, so I combined them into one chapter. The fact of my womanhood and resulting treatment caused me to perceive almost every situation differently from American men my age. And then, I added a few needs that I felt Maslow neglected or did not name (i.e. transportation).

My contract with the University said I would abide by and observe the laws of the 'sharia', the religious rules that evolved from the Koran. There are many variations when translators transliterate words for which there is no good translation such as Sharia which is sometimes spelled 'Shari'ah', or Koran which is sometimes spelled 'Kuran' or 'Qur'an'. This was a common cause of miscommunication between people using the English alphabet to spell words spoken in Arabic. Therefore, I operated for two years under these Quranic laws;

<u>Article 50</u> **Statutes Governing the Employment of Non-Saudis with the University of Riyadh.**

The contractee is committed to follow the present and future procedures, laws and instructions in force in the Kingdom of Saudi Arabia, and he and his dependents should respect the habits and customs of the Kingdom, particularly as regards the non-violation of religious ethics and non-interference in politics.

Article 53

The contract is terminated before expiry in the following cases:

g. Disciplinary dismissal by decree of the disciplinary council (Investigation and Disciplinary Board)

h. Dismissal for the public good.

i. The passing of a sharia (religious law) sentence upon the contractee, or his sentencing for dishonorable or dishonest conduct.

I included passages from the Koran in each chapter. I chose suras (chapters) which I felt expressed an idea or conflict which had an impact on life there.

W. Montgomery Watt (1961) points out that it is chiefly for marrying and inheritance that the Quran gives precise rules . . ."

He goes on to say;

> "In actual life what is commonly called 'Islamic law' produces something very like the mores of a primitive people. Since it was not exactly law at all, as that is usually understood, it is referred to here as the Shari'ah. It should be noted that the word shari'ah properly means 'revelation' in general and is not restricted to the legal aspect of revelation."

I agree that the shari'ah is primitive, especially as it is applied by the mutawahs (religious police) who have the right and power to hit people with their staffs if they are displeased with their behavior, as well as to arrest arbitrarily. They can force men to pray and if they resist can force them to sign a papers that say "I am a sinner". Now that is primitive!

The following are from *The Quran* translated by Abdallah Yousuf Ali in 1931.

Sura XVI Section 2
It is he who sends down
Rain from the sky;
From it ye drink,
And out of it (grows)
The vegetation on which
Ye feed your cattle.

Verse 11
With it, He produces
For you corn, olives,
Date-palms, grapes,
And every kind of fruit:
Verily in this is a Sign
For those who give thought.

When I got up that first morning in Riyadh, my flat mate offered me bottled water. I knew not to drink the tap water until I knew it was potable, because of long years of association with Mexican border towns.

Just before I left Long Beach, there was pressure from some health devotees to use bottled water, as they thought the tap water was polluted. But I had just shrugged my shoulders and said, "Damn it, this is going too far. I'm supposed to trust my Water and Power Plant people. I'll drink tap water."

In Riyadh, I did not trust the Water Plant people. Mostly, it was not their fault. Firstly, the water pipe system underground was built for a much smaller city. Every time that they extended the pipes, it changed the water pressure, so bacteria could seep through from the outside, "back-siphoning" they called it. In some cases through poor planning and engineering, sewer pipes paralleled the water pipes at a not very great distance. Many apartments and villas controlled their own water supply by having water tanks on their roofs. The water pressure was so erratic, that many dwellings had a ground storage tank which they filled when the water pressure was high, then pumping it to their roof tank. They could then use their own filter or purification system. Most of us never trusted that the tap water was bacteria free enough to drink safely.

Another one of the main hazards of tap water was its calcium content.

The way that calcium content is measured is how many milliliters per liter of water. Comparatively, Riyadh had 200 ml. per liter compared with London which has 80; Liverpool which has 20 which is considered ideal and bottled water, one brand which had 68 ml. per liter and a scarcer brand which had 16 ml. per liter. Calcium plus a combination of dietary factors produces one of the highest incidences of kidney stones anywhere in the world. A plastic bottle containing 1½ liters cost approximately 65 cents in 1980. Some people bought them by the case which contained twelve bottles and cost $7.80. At first, I, too, bought this expensive liquid which was more expensive than the $1.40 gasoline at home in California at the time. But when I discovered that I could buy a 'Jeri can' made from plastic which would hold 20 liters for only 2 riyals or 65 cents, I decided to do that. Either way, they were too heavy for me to carry by myself from the store to the flat. It required a male and his car. Why not get the cheaper one? And so I did. I used a piece of plastic tubing from the hospitals lab to siphon it into more utilitarian sized bottles for keeping in the refrigerator. The stores which sold the water for jeri cans were called 'healthy water' factories or plants. They filled the jeri can with a hose and nozzle just like the gas pump in the USA. The first time I went, the proprietor filled a glass and stood over me until I sampled his wares and pronounced the water good. On subsequent occasions, I declined to sample since I saw that he offered the same glass to everyone.

The following is the story of Moses making his way out of Egypt as told in the Koran.

Sura XXVIII Verse 22
Then, when he turned his face
Toward (the land of) Maydan,
He said: "I do hope
That my Lord will show me
The smooth and straight Path."

Verse 23
And when he arrived at
The watering (place) in Maydan,
He found there a group
Of men watering (their flocks),
And beside them he found
Two women who were keeping
Back (their flocks). He said:
"What is the matter with you?"

They said: "We cannot water
(Our flocks) until the shepherds
Take back (their flocks):
And our father is
A very old man."

Verse 24
So he watered (their flocks)
For them: then he turned back
To the shade, and said:
"O my Lord!
Truly am I
In (desperate) need
Of any good
That Thou dost send me!"

Verse 25
Afterwards one of the (damsels)
Came (back) to him, walking
Bashfully. She said: "My father
Invites thee for having watered
(Our flocks) for us." So when
He came to him and narrated
The story, he said:
"Fear thou not: (well) has thou
Escaped from unjust people."

Verse 26
Said one of the (damsels):
"O my (dear) father! Engage
Him on wages: truly the best
Of men for thee to employ is
The (man) who is strong and trusty."

Verse 27
He said: "I intend to wed
One of these my daughters
To thee, on condition that
Thou serve me for eight years;

But if thou complete ten years,
It will be (grace) from thee.
But I intend not to place
Thee under difficulty:
Thou wilt find me
Indeed, if God wills,
One of the righteous."

Verse 28
He said: "Be that (the agreement)
Between me and thee:
I fulfill, let there be
No ill-will to me.
Be God a witness
To what we say."

There are many parallels between Qur'anic stories and Bible stories. The reader may like to compare the Islamic version with Exodus 2 verse 15-22.

Many ancient wells remain in the peninsula. An Arabist acquaintance guessed some to be 4000 years old. During my term there, I visited seven ancient wells. One could easily get a feeling of stepping back into the scenes described in Sura XXVIII. Many of these wells are still in use by Bedouin shepherds. On one, I saw apparatus for raising the water to the surface. Near another, there were pieces of bright colored plastic rope about which indicated to me that in the recent past, water had been raised. From the surface down, perhaps 12 feet, the insides of the wells I saw were surfaced with dressed stones measuring between one and two feet square which were closely fitted around the opening, and mostly still intact. Where the facing stones ended beneath the earth's surface, the remainder of the wells appeared to be of solid stone. In some the water levels were low enough for me to see the marks of some ancient drill. I wondered at the engineering feats of the ancients. In one case, about 100 kilometers (about 62 miles, from Riyadh, a village was still situated ½ kilometer from the well which was still in use. There was an oblong tank fashioned from the local stone and mortar which apparently was still used for watering by camel drivers. It had the old wooden apparatus with a cogged wheel for raising the precious liquid to the surface.

Sura LXXII Verse 16
(And God's Message is):
"If they (the Pagans)

Had (only) remained
On the (right) Way,
We should certainly have
Bestowed on them Rain
In Abundance.

Twice during my second year, the King declared a holiday from work and school in order to pray for rain. According to desert standards, they had been having a drought. So all government offices and agencies were closed. This holiday was announced in the late evening on the Arabic TV News. The English speakers knew nothing of it; so of course, we had gone to work to find no students.

Pepsi Cola was the most common beverage both out on the work sites as well as in restaurants and at parties. The Pepsi Company had that country sewed up as Coca Cola was forbidden. The reason for its prohibition was that it had a bottling company in Israel. Any product or company that was made in or used by the Israelis was on a 'black list' in Saudi Arabia and not allowed to be imported. For a time, there was a beverage called Kaki Cola which some people said was really a Saudi cover for Coca Cola, but it disappeared soon after my arrival. Pepsi improved its plant and had a street named after it, at least it was so named by Westerners who called it Pepsi Road. There were many small ways where daily I was reminded of the ancient conflict between Jews and Arabs.

Artificially sweetened beverages were not produced in the Kingdom. In the commissary for the American government employees, they could be found. It was a great treat to be offered an artificially sweetened drink because of its rarity. The Saudis like their sugar. I could find saccharin in pharmacies, but on only one occasion did I ever find 'Sweet and Low' in a local store. When I returned to buy more, it was all gone. One of the rules my first flat mate gave me was,"When you see something you especially want or use, buy all of it because you probably won't find it again." She was right.

One of my first memories of being served a beverage outside my flat was when I visited the carpet 'souq' or market with a pretty blond friend. She was well known there from previous visits as she was planning to buy a couple of carpets before completing her contract and returning home to England. When we walked down the covered alley, several young men ran out from one shop calling to her and to me to come in and sit down for tea. We consulted each other and decided it was OK since we were together. They seated us on piles of expensive Persian carpets. From somewhere, we knew not where, appeared a tray with a teapot and several tiny glasses with handles. Our hosts poured out the heavily sugared hot tea. Obviously, they were thoroughly enjoying entertaining these two foreign females. I was not aware at the time what trouble we could have been in had a 'mutawah', a religious policeman have happened along and found men and women socializing together in public. The tray was placed on the floor, and tea glasses were passed around. We did not buy any carpets that evening. But we drank a lot of tea among many admiring glances.

This kind of hot tea was served in many offices while one waited to talk to the head man. Unfortunately, this quaint and pleasant custom was on the decrease as the foreign population increased in the city. During my two years there, I observed this change. In the street, during working hours, I saw servants carrying enormous trays full of pots and glasses to unknown destinations.

When I went to a restaurant in a hotel where it was safe for men and women to dine together with no fear of the mutawahs, the most common beverage to be served aside from the perennial bottled water was a mixture called 'Saudi Champagne'. Since all alcoholic beverages were forbidden, people did all sorts of things to substitute, to give that feeling of drinking. 'Saudi Champagne' was one such simulation. If involved pouring a bottle of apple juice and a bottle of Perrier water at the same time into a pitcher of fresh fruit pieces. It did taste remarkably like champagne and gave the feeling of graciousness and celebration we associate with that 'special' beverage.

Another simulation was the 'phony beer, 'plastic beer,' also designated as 'non-alcoholic beer'. It is a malt beverage without alcohol to keep in compliance with Islamic law. I found it nearly as refreshing as the **real** stuff without the woozy boozy feeling I have after three bottles of alcoholic beer. Our drink called 'Near Beer' was unavailable for a time, until the suppliers decided to remove the word 'beer' from the label. Then the Saudis allowed it to be sold under the name NEAR. The only problem for me with 'plastic beer' was the difficulty of carrying it to the bus from the store in that thirsty climate, balancing a six pack or two on my lap on the bus and then carrying it two blocks to the flat. It felt good in hot weather which was most of the time. However, I gave myself a 'beer' treat only on special thirsty occasions.

Sura V Verse 93
Ye who believe!
Intoxicants and gambling,
(Dedication of) stones,
And (divination by) arrows,
Are an abomination, --
Of Satan's handiwork:

Eschew such (abominations),
That ye may prosper.

Verse 94
Satan's plan is (but)
To excite enmity and hatred
Between you, with intoxicants
And gambling, and hinder you
From the remembrance
Of God, and from prayer:
Will ye not then abstain?

An American government consultant on food purity assisted in efforts to keep pork and alcohol out of the Kingdom. They allowed .1% alcohol, so his job was to test English plum puddings, mouthwash, vinegar, soft drinks, etc.

Of course, many people were not satisfied by non-alcoholic products, no matter what they were. So a big hobby with Westerners, which meant anybody from Europe of our side of the Atlantic, was to make their own beverage; wine, beer, ale, or *sediki* which in Arabic means 'friend' but in the Saudi brewers' world it meant grain alcohol. It was the locally distilled beverage.

Before I embark on accounts of these local brews, I want to recount how the British and American military and government employees got their alcoholic allowance. For Americans, it was shipped into Customs in boxes labeled TEA. The British shipped theirs in packages labeled FURNITURE. In the American community, one of the frequent topics of conversation was the past, future and current TEA SHIPMENTS. When the shipment came in, it was as good as money, unless you wanted to drink it. Each month, each person employed directly by the US government was entitled to some, if they were in an organization that was a member of the 'Recreation' group which received the TEA shipment. The amount differed with each shipment. It might include one bottle each of gin, vodka, rum or scotch. They could be traded, borrowed, given or sold. My first year, I was too nervous over the consequences which would undoubtedly be jail so I seldom drank. I had perhaps ten drinks that whole year. By my second year, I felt more 'at home' if that is possible in a place where severe punishment is an ever-present threat, and I did take a drink when it was offered. I never had to worry about drinking and driving, and driving was the time when most drinkers were apprehended and jailed. Also, my second year I had found a group of compatible friends.

For me that involved a bit of drink, not excessive, just a bit, enough to keep my anxiety level up.

Reportedly, during my first year, liquor could be bought on the 'black market' for about 280-300 Saudi riyals per bottle. That was about $84.00 at the exchange rate then. But at the beginning of my second year, the price had gone up to $400 Saudi riyals, approximately $116.00 per fifth, if one could find a seller at all. Illegal liquor, which it all was, had nearly dried up. One of the rumors I heard about why this happened was that previously, most liquor shipments, aside from TEA and FURNITRE shipments, came up from the Yemeni boarder. But after the AWACs were flying and spying, the liquor smuggling was virtually brought to a halt. Prices went up. I met some American AWAC pilots and reported this tale to them. They just laughed and did not answer. That reaction made me believe this story.

WINE-my favorite! This I missed more than any other beverage since we had such lovely cheap wine in California. The first homemade wine I tasted in Saudi Arabia was still a little raw so that the taste gave me a bad impression. I did not feel too well afterwards either, but during my second year, I formed a friendship with a man who had formerly been stationed in Rome for several years. He regularly bemoaned this lack of fine wine. I asked him if he would consider making some himself. I would not have considered doing it myself since most of my neighbors were Saudis and other Middle Eastern Muslims. He said, "Ok, if I knew how." His years in Rome had made him think it was too complex for a non-vintner. But I knew some real 'klutzes' who had made some pretty good stuff, so I decided it couldn't be that difficult. I told my friend I would ask around about how to start. So I did. It was so simple that it was no surprise that half the Americans I knew were making their own. This is the recipe we used:

1. Buy a plastic Jeri can.
2. Buy a case of natural, unsweetened grape juice.
3. Put a kilo of granulated sugar in the bottom of the Jeri can along with 2 or 3 tablespoons of bread yeast.
4. Pour in the grape juice.
5. Agitate the Jeri can until the sugar is absorbed or at least wetted.
6. Wait for or five days until it bubbles with the plastic Jeri cover laid on but not screwed down. It is best to make it in the kitchen or bath as it may bubble over.
7. Wait another month.

8. Rack it – or in a laywoman's terms use a piece of plastic tubing to siphon it into the same bottles which have been sterilized. Do not disturb the sediment in the bottom while siphoning.
9. Store in the bottles for another two weeks at a minimum.
10. Drink it.

This is the simplest recipe I hear or used. The first batch wasn't too bad, though my ex-Roman friend thought it much too sweet, so he put very little sugar into the second batch. It was OK too. The only bad time during the whole procedure was when we went into the medical supply store in my neighborhood to get the plastic tubing. A policeman followed us in. I knew this policeman by sight since he managed the traffic at the corner where I frequently waited for the bus. It was obvious that he knew me too. His presence made me nervous since I was not married to my friend and our being together was actually illegal under Saudi law so I whispered to him that I would go to the nearby grocery store. I left him to get the tubing. When I arrived at the checkout stand, there was my policeman watching me to see what I purchased. Fortunately, it was just tuna and coffee, nothing for wine making. My blood pressure was up by the time we drove away from the area. I'd already seen the inside of the women's jail before while visiting inmates.

During my last few months, an American government employee, who had been arrested for receiving a wine-making kit in the mail, had been acquitted of the charges of making alcoholic beverages when his wife went to the *souq*, the market, and bought all the equipment contained in the kit to prove to the judge these same things were available locally. This poor man had been the unsuspecting recipient of the winemaking kit sent to him unsolicited by his mother via the APO. Some Americans took this as a warning and harbinger of further repressions.

Real beer and ale were beverages with which I had little experience there. I had only second-hand reports and hearsay. Bottles would explode during brewing and leave a terrible incriminating smell. I never tasted homemade beer. I always feared that home brews of whatever sort might have toxins in them that commercial products had filtered out.

Sediki, 'my friend' was just pure grain beverage that had been distilled. Some people liked it a great deal and mixed it with cordials, or just orange juice for 'screwdriver'. Close to the time I arrived in Saudi Arabia, one American company compound had had a commercial still run privately by a resident. Apparently, he sold his sediki to the wrong person. The police raided his house. The still was confiscated and he was deported along with several others. The manager of that company had his passport appropriated and held hostage.

Because they were forbidden, intoxicants occupied a great deal of everyone's conversation, the same way marijuana did for Americans at home. Those that didn't were judgmental of those that did. Those that did discussed how, where, and when they did it, as well as the penalties if caught. The penalties were fairly severe. For Americans, it meant deportation immediately. For some citizens of less powerful countries, it meant long jail terms. If any American employer did not care for their employees, they too might rot in prison for a long time.

The *Saudi Gazette*, a daily English language newspaper printed in Saudi Arabia, had an article called 'You'll Treasure this Spain', May 20, 1982 which shows the humorous lengths to which Saudis go to discuss alcoholic beverages while at the same time fooling the censors. It read as follows:

> The only slight drawback is that
> Again like France, Spain is patriotically
> Proud of its grape juice products, almost
> To the exclusion of other country's imports.

I felt the Saudis had misperceived the Prophet's original intent. Surely he meant for the fluids of life to be enjoyed in health. In an antique store, I purchased a primitively worked little piece of copper with some Arabic words crudely inscribed on it. I got many Arabs to try to read it to me. We turned it upside down and right side up. We tried reading it backwards with a mirror. I got religious interpretations, secular interpretations. Finally, a man from Amman, Jordan read it and said it was an old saying in Jordan, "Drink of happiness and health." This response was given whenever a drink was offered. Because he knew the saying, he was able to decipher the calligraphy. I felt sure this saying was in keeping with the intent of the Prophet.

REFERENCES:

Ali, Abdallah Yousef (1931) *The Quran*. Egypt.

Maslow, Abraham (1968) *Toward a Psychology of Being*. New York: G. Van Nostrand and Company.

Watt, W. Montgomery (1961) *Islam and the Interpretation of Society*. London: Routledge & Kegan Paul Ltd.

3

FOOD

Guess what? No vitamins! Anyway, not the kind I used such as stress tablets, brewers yeast, desiccated liver. However, multivitamins like Therigran-M were available in pharmacies. For three years previously, I had been an ovo-lacto vegetarian which means I would eat eggs and dairy products. I decided not to attempt to maintain that regime in a country about which I knew so little of their food habits. I wanted to be open to enjoy my adventure. I would be under enough restriction without adding self-imposed ones.

Sura V Verse 2

Lawful unto you (for food)
Are all four-footed animals,
With the exceptions named:
But the animals of the chase
Are forbidden while ye
Are in the Sacred Precincts
Or in pilgrimage garb:
For God doth command
According to His Will and Plan.

Verse 4

Forbidden to you (for food)
Are: dead meat, blood,
The flesh of swine, and that

On which hath been invoked
The name of other than God;
That which hath been
Killed by strangling,
Or by a violent blow,
Or by a headlong fall,
Or by being gored to death;
That which hath been (partly)
Eaten by a wild animal;
Unless ye are able
To slaughter it (in due form);
That which is sacrificed
On stone (altars);
(Forbidden) also is the division
(Of meat) by raffling
With arrows: that is impiety.

This meant that much of our American meat was forbidden. No wringing of necks of chicken! Prohibitions against pork are mentioned no less than eight times. Animals of the chase in the Prophet's time included gazelles, doves, foxes and pheasants. Those were forbidden foods while the pilgrims were in Mecca in the area of the Grand Mosque. The 'pilgrim garb' will be described in the next chapter on clothing. For most of the world's people, any meat that is cooked is considered 'dead meat'. However, the meaning in the Koran is meat of animals not specifically killed according to the correct procedure. Correct killing involves slitting the animal's throat and hanging it up by its hind legs to drain off the blood. For example, if a farm animal is hit by a car and killed, Americans will usually dress it and cook it. Forbidden in Islam! No 'blood sausage' for them as they let it all drain away losing all that protein and iron. At Hajj, the pilgrimage time, on the day of 'sacrifice' when every family at the pilgrimage place kills a sheep, reportedly the ground is slick and slippery with blood as it drains out of the slaughtered animals unto the ground. As a non-Muslim I was not allowed into Mecca to observe this. In the days of the Prophet, there was no gun powder and there were no 'stun-guns' such as our meat packers use. In the supermarkets, much of the frozen meat came from New Zealand, Australia and South America. It was doubtful that the Saudi government monitored the killing methods of these countries, and Muslims I knew did eat meat that had been shot or killed by falcons.

Sura VI Verse 141

It is He who produceth
Gardens, with trellises
And without, and dates,
And tilith with produce
Of all kinds, and olives
And pomegranates,
Similar (in kind)
And different (in variety):
Eat of their fruit
In their season, but render
The dues that are proper
On that day that the harvest
Is gathered. But waste not
By excess: for God
Loveth not the wasters.

The harvest season is an all year round affair in areas with enough water for crops. I never saw or heard of any harvest festival in Saudi Arabia. Some other Muslim countries do observe this seasonal ritual to 'render the dues to the gods of harvest'.

The Saudis that I knew apparently did not know or decided to ignore the warning about God not loving wasters. So much wasting of food as well as other things, I never saw as much as I saw there. It seemed a ritual to fill a plate to heaping while at the buffet, and then take only a few bites. I saw this occur at banquets, wedding parties, office parties, in homes and at 'goat grabs', an event where a whole roasted goat on a huge tray of rice was placed on the carpet as the entrée with plates of fruit and salad ringing it. It was all to be eaten with the fingers. This practice of leaving a filled plate appeared to be a contradiction between the culture and the observance of the religion.

Sura VI Verse 146

For those who followed
The Jewish Law, We forbade
Every (animal) with
Undivided hoof,
And We forbade them
The fat of the ox
And the sheep, except
What adheres to their backs

Or their entrails,
Or is mixed up
With a bone:
This is recompense
For their willful disobedience;
For We are True
(In Our Ordinances).

The Prophet was giving newer laws than those already given to the Jews. The Koran is supposedly the word of God hence the use of the first person plural, 'We'. Muslims believe that Jewish and Christian prophets were also speaking for God. Mohamed came with a later message which superseded the earlier ones. He was giving newer laws about the 'undivided hoof'. Camel, rabbit and hare which were forbidden to Jews, the Prophet updated to make them lawful for Muslims.

At Saudi dinners, guests of honor, of which I was occasionally one, had liver, heart, and kidney heaped unto their plate regardless of whether they wanted it or not. I believe this had to do with their interpretation of 'fat adhering to the entrails'. Bone marrow was also presented as a delicacy. However, since a whole roasted sheep or chicken was the commonest way to serve meat, it was difficult to get at the marrow without seeming like a cavewoman, perhaps breaking the femur over my knee. Soup spoons were provided at these events, but no knives and forks.

I was privileged to attend a lecture at the Riyadh Dieticians' Association given by a surgeon who frequently removed enormous 'stag horn' renal stones. You can imagine what that name represents. Kidney stones in the shape of a deer horn form in the vessels which normally drain the urine. This surgeon's task was to remove them. We occasionally get such formations in people in our culture, too but basically, our diet causes different problems. These formations were a result of particular features in the Saudi diet according to surgeon Peter Bond. Firstly, as noted in the last chapter, they got too much calcium in the water. Secondly, the Saudi diet is extremely high in sugar from sweetened tea, Pepsi and other sugared drinks in addition to many sweets. Their food is also high in calcium as they regularly eat 'laban' which is like our yogurt but has more fat so it is the consistency of sour cream, this latter which was not available in the stores by the way. The diet is also high in protein from the 'laban' and meat. For centuries they have been used to rationing their fluid intake in the desert. Food habits die hard as we American dieters know, so this continues as a feature of their diet. A further complication is the low fiber content. Vegetables grow poorly in hot dry climates and those that did, frequently wilted before arriving at the market. They imported fruits and vegetables from Jordan and Egypt but they were expensive, so that source of fiber was limited. Natural bran which we get in so many of our grain foods was refined out in Saudi Arabia. That probably came about as a climatic and cultural phenomenon. Packing bran on a camel as compared to packing refined white flour which has more food value would have probably made the camel driver choose white over brown flour since it would provide more energy per weight and space. Most bread was white. Saudis also got little sunlight. We normally think that in a land where trees are few, sunlight would be plentiful, which it is, if a person ventured out into it. They did not and I did not either if there was a convenient air-conditioner or spot of shade. The fierce heat kept everyone in quiet shaded places. Of course, the bodies of the women are completely covered so even their faces seldom get sun. The men's head clothes also kept nearly all the sun away from them as well. This combination of high calcium, high protein, high sugar, low fiber, low fluid intake and little sunlight produced poor calcium metabolization. That resulted in renal problems according to the surgeon.

Groceries in modern Riyadh seemed very costly to me. I invited some friends over one evening. New England boiled dinner is a no-fail meal even for the most primitive kitchen, which ours was. No, I take it back. It had a refrigerator, and running water. That's not really primitive. When I went to buy some cheap roast beef, it cost me fifty riyals, approximately seventeen dollars at the exchange rate then. It would have cost approximately five dollars in Long Beach in 1980. That was pretty expensive for a 'cheap' piece of meat, but it adequately fed eight of us. By the time I bought and prepared everything, it cost fifty dollars which was a lot in 1980 for a thrifty person to spend. There wasn't even a liquor bill. I did not entertain very often at those prices and with those inconveniences. I estimate I could have served the same meal at home a lot more conveniently for approximately twenty-five dollars and served a gallon of red wine, too.

Shopping in Riyadh was a real adventure, one of the only safe adventures available. The fruit and vegetable souqs were of several varieties; small, medium, large, comprehensive and specialized. Supermarkets carried the same varieties as the small shops on the street at similar prices. But the produce in the small shops was usually more abundant, in better condition and not wrapped in plastic pre-counted quantities. Because the small shops did not have refrigeration, leafy vegetables, which were few, wilted quickly. A trip to the vegetable souq meant for me, a five to ten minute wait for the bus two blocks from our flat. Then a five minute ride and a three block walk from the bus to the shops. Then I walked back again carrying perhaps fifteen pounds of produce in my nylon shopping bag. I made this trip infrequently.

For me, another problem was the situation of having to share a refrigerator, so I couldn't buy much at one time.

There was also a wholesale produce market. Once, I bought a case of apples there with my flat-mate, but they spoiled even more rapidly there than they do in California. Like many hot climates, the apples were not so good initially. With the lack of humidity, they wither rapidly.

Early in my stay, I heard that it was necessary to wash all fruits and vegetables in soapy water as human feces were much used as fertilizer on farms in the Middle East. So each trip was followed by stacking the produce in the sink and running it full of cold water and detergent, then letting them soak for twenty minutes. Hopefully, this destroyed all fecal born microbes.

Ah! The spice souq! That was a lovely place. It was near the incense souq. Someone quoted someone as saying "The best and the worst things about the Middle East are the smells." I found that to be quite true. I've always been an olfactory person. The spice souq was both an olfactory and visual experience. It could be tactile, too, if I got close to other shoppers and got pinched or squeezed. The olfactory aspect was distinguishable from half a block away when I began to smell the cardamom, curry powder, turmeric and new spices I've never smelled before. When it came into my sight, I saw the black clothed, veiled merchants sitting on the cement walkway behind huge baskets of their wares. The baskets contained powders in colors of saffron, yellow, orange, amber, ocher and brick red. In a more modern section of the same souq, men sold similar spices in wooden bins.

I usually bought bread from a Yemeni bakery about four blocks from our flat. The dough was mixed in a big electric mixer, but baked in the traditional way by sliding the flat round piece of dough into onto the hot oven floor with a long wooden spatula and removing it the same way. However, the oven was heated by a modern gas flame, not camel dung as I had anticipated. This whole wheat bread was lovely delicious stuff, unavailable anywhere else in the city. I could buy dark wheat bread at one of the new supermarkets that opened halfway through my stay, but since it was not wrapped, I could never be sure how many people had handled it. It was the Christian bread squeezers I was afraid of since I could be sure that the good Muslims had washed their hands at least five times per day for praying.

Customers could buy their own sheep to slaughter at any sheep souq of which there were several. These souqs consisted of blocks and blocks of crudely constructed pens. The shepherd usually has his campfire right beside his pen. In the butcher souq, a customer could watch his sheep being slaughtered and buy just part or you could buy almost the same cuts we have already packaged in the supermarket. That is the only place I ever purchased any meat, though I found it fascinating to see a freshly killed sheep's eyes staring at me from the skinned head as it lay among other cuts of meat in the butcher souq. I was surprised at how few flies there were in that souq. It made me wonder what kind of insecticide they might have sprayed on the meat as I'd never seen such a prolific use of insecticide. One of my colleagues at the University described for me the time when she walked into a room where the cleaning girls had all the aerosol spray containers they could find, approximately thirty. They were taking turns spraying and smelling to sample as many as possible.

I lived in two different flats with four different flat mates during my two years. I experienced a variety of kitchen arrangements. My first kitchen reminded me of kitchens I had seen in England where much of the countertop had no cupboards underneath, just open space. The second kitchen was even less well equipped with counter space. In both cases, the stoves had no pilot. We lit the burners with a special flint gun. The stove was fueled from a propane tank which sat on the floor next to the stove and frequently ran out of fuel at inconvenient times. Each kitchen had a two basin sink, stove, and refrigerator as equipment. The drain hole in the floor was covered by a round of aluminum so we were not subjected to constant gurglings as the sink emptied. Both kitchens had poor lighting. Each kitchen had only one electrical outlet. The fuse blew each time the refrigerator went on at the same time I was using the fry pan. The walls were either tile or plaster into which we were forbidden to put hooks or nails. These were the University Housing Rules. So, all together, cooking was not a pleasure. Much of that lack came from having to share all facilities and storage with another grown woman.

Middle Easterners women seldom accompanied their men to restaurants for dinners or celebrations. As Saudi women were forbidden to be seen by *non-sohbah* or *maharram* men, most of the parties I attended were women's parties. These two terms refer to men who were forbidden to women by their relationship status. The main feature of women's parties was the food. I would be invited to arrive about 8 pm. Usually the hostess would arrange for a relative to come round and pick up the wheel-less women. I would always be picked up at least one half hour later than promised, sometimes two hours, so I would arrive at the party place between 9 and 10 pm. Most houses had a seldom used front parlor similar to our Victorian house arrangements. The guests would all be relieved of their black cloaks called *abayas*, their purses or other wraps and then they would be seated in the parlor where chairs and sofas seemed always to be pushed back against the walls in a copy of the royal family's audience room. Then the hostess or her servant would come around and serve Saudi coffee which is ground cardamom served from a specially shaped Arabic coffee pot which has a large spout into which was stuffed a bit of palm fiber which strained the coffee as it was poured into minuscule cups. After 3 or 4 cups, they were collected and small glasses with handles were served full of the ever present sweetened hot tea or the lovely sweetened mint tea. Sometime during all this beverage serving, a family member would come round carrying an elaborate basket of foil wrapped Swiss chocolates. Many guests would take several, though each was as large as a small candy bar. They would tuck away these extras to take home. Because the quality of the candy bar was so good, it would begin to melt the moment it was in contact with body temperatures. Messy! About 11 or 11:30 pm the meal would be served. In my journal I described it like this:

> We all went into the dining room where a table which would seat eight was absolutely covered with platters of food, two turkeys, chicken pieces, a giant birthday cake of two tiers with a section of 6 inches or air between tiers, Middle Eastern rice with lots of nuts and raisins, salad, cold sliced meat, meat filled dumplings, meat filled pastries, flan and so much more I can't name it all, just to feed about 12 of us. Then she served the sweetened tea again.

Seldom were any women seen in restaurants, except in "Western" style hotels so most of my 'dine-out' experiences were there. However, on one or two occasions, I sat down to be served in restaurants run by Lebanese. The food was delicious, plentiful and served as a very leisurely pace. Hors d'oeuvres usually consisted of black olives, green onions, radishes, and hummus which is ground seasoned chickpeas also called Garbanzo Beans, with flat unleavened bread to scoop it up. The meat courses would follow with kebabs or steak or fish; then more salad, Turkish coffee and pastry.

Such restaurants had special "family sections' where women were urged to sit. Single men and groups of men without women were forbidden to sit there. This allowed the Saudi women to be served there and not break their "no face seeing" rule. Most fast-food places did have a sitting section, but not for women. In some places, women were absolutely forbidden to sit down. If the mutawah appeared, they always demanded that the women leave to comply with the Saudi "no mixture of the sexes" rule.

In the lobbies of the "Western" style hotels, we could have coffee and other legal beverages served while we sat on sofas. *Mutawahs* seldom policed there. The waiters would walk around and take orders from the various seating areas.

On one occasion, I was fortunate enough to be asked to join a dinner party in the most expensive hotel, paid for by a leading American capitalist. I recorded it thus:

"I had duck liver pate' for starters at 20 riyals (^$6.50) then *hamoor*, a common Persian Gulf fish for 48 riyals ($16.00) and then a sweet for another 20 riyals."

I thought that rather expensive in 1981 but I wasn't paying.

Saudi mealtimes were on a schedule different from ours. Most Middle-Easterners I knew came to work without breakfast. About 8:30 or 9 am, shortly after arriving, they would have a snack at their desk. This usually consisted of sesame covered breadsticks with a glass of tea. Their tea looked like dirty milk to me. I watched our secretary make it many times. She put three scoops of sugar, two heaping scoops of non-dairy creamer and a teabag into a glass, and then poured the remainder full of hot water. I could never bring myself to taste this revolting looking mixture. However, this was their daily morning fare. They would not eat again until they arrived home after work about 2:30 pm, at which time they would have their big meal of the day, unless an evening party was anticipated. After this big afternoon meal, they would nap until approximately 4:30 pm when the *souqs* reopened or afternoon prayer call, which ever came first. The evening meal on a regular day would be served approximately 9:30 pm. They seldom went to bed until after midnight, children as well as adults. I could hear children playing in the hallway outside our flat until 12 o'clock on many weeknights. Since most work started at 7:30 am, they needed that afternoon siesta.

Lack of breast feeding was a great problem there where the birthrate was so high; 7 ½ live births per woman. As in most developed countries, upper and middle class women knew the advantages of breast feeding; convenience, temperature control of the milk, reduced possibility of contamination, nutrients, and immunological properties of mother's milk. It was the uneducated, which made up approximately 80%of women who preferred infant formulas which they frequently diluted to half strength with contaminated water; hence, babies were frequently malnourished. They were brought to the clinics with severe diarrhea. Part of all these problems could have been remedied with educational television programs, but in my two years I did not see one TV program on nutrition. Children's nutrition was not yet a priority. I was told on several occasions by Muslim women, that the Koran admonishes women to cease nursing by the time the child reaches two years of age. After diligent searching, I was unable to find this injunction.

One other malnutrition problem was that female children had a higher rate of deprivation because when meals were served, men ate first. Then when a boy became five, they were allowed to eat with the men. Women ate next and female children ate last. A friend who worked for the United Nations described the experience of sitting down to a meal in a small city. The men and boys ate while a female child was allowed to play around the periphery. She was not allowed to approach the food trays on the floor in the center of the circle.

Male children are allowed to nurse approximately 6 to 12 months longer than females. Males end up having preferential nutrition throughout life. This may have some effect in the female passivity that I saw in all strata of Saudi life. When a person is weak and tired, they usually do not have the will to assert their rights.

REFERENCES:

Ali, Abdallah Yousef (1931) *The Quran*. Egypt.

4

CLOTHES

Sura 33 Verse 59
*Prophet! Tell
Thy wives and daughters
And the believing women,
That they should caste
Their outer garments over
Their persons (when abroad):
That is most convenient
That they should be known
(As such) and not molested.
And God is Oft-Forgiving,
Most Merciful.*

Sura 24 Verse 31
*And say to the believing women
That they should lower
Their gaze and guard
Their modesty; that they
Should not display their
Beauty and ornaments except
What (must ordinarily) appear
Thereof, that they should*

Draw their veils over
Their bosoms and not display
Their beauty except
To their husbands, their fathers
Their husbands' fathers, their sons,
Their husbands' sons,
Their brothers or their brothers' sons,
Or their sisters' sons,
Or their women, or their slaves
Whom their right hand possess, or male servants
Free of physical needs – (This line refers to eunuchs.)
Or small children who have no sense of the shame
Of sex, and that they
Should not strike their feet
In order to draw attention
To their hidden ornaments.

In the Koran there seems to be less about clothing than many other aspects, yet in Saudi Arabia, there seemed to be more preoccupation with clothing, especially that of women, than almost any other topic except oil or money. From the previous two verses they had devised the extremity of keeping their women covered in black from head to foot. To me, this seemed cruel and unusual punishment, to be obliged to wear the most heat absorbing color in this hottest of all climates. Why? I have not been able to find a plausible answer. The *Koran* does not specify black. Abdullah Yousef Ali, the translator and commentator of my *Koran* (1931) made a footnote to the following effect:

> The object was not to restrict the liberty of women, but to protect them from harm and molestation under the condition then existing in Medina. In the East and in the West a distinctive public dress of some sort or another has always been a badge of honor and distinction, both among men and women. Assyrian law in its palmiest days enjoined the veiling of married women and forbade the veiling of slaves and women of ill fame: see *Cambridge Ancient History III.* 107.

Beck and Keddie (1978) reason it out like this:

Traditionally limited to the urban upper and middle classes,
severe veiling and seclusion were signs that a man could afford
to have servants do the household shopping and errands and
that he occupied an economic position that allowed him to
protect the honor of his family from abuse. Recently, veiling and
seclusion have become much more complex social phenomena.
While the wealthier classes educated in the Western ways have
increasingly abandoned veiling and seclusion, these practices,
ironically have spread among the lower middle and lower classes
. . . This was partly a sign of status – the lower classes imitating
the bazaar bourgeoisie, the men showing themselves capable of
'inconspicuous consumption'. p. 8

In Saudi Arabia, veiling included all women. The Bedouin women wore
their own distinctive veil which allowed the eyes to show, while urban women
wear the cloth that covers their entire head.

J.E. Cirlot (1962) indicates that the veil has different significance in the
following definition:

In addition to partaking of the generic symbolism of fabrics,
the veil signifies the concealment of certain aspects of the truth
or of the deity . . . p. 379.

The most amusing explanation I found for the veiling phenomenon was
by Muhammad Abdul-Rauf (1973):

A woman is a sweet creature and can easily be seductive. Her
gaze can be seductive; so is her voice, her gait, her bosom, her
legs and the form of her feet and the shape of her ankles. If you
leave a sweet thing uncovered, you will be inviting swarms of
dirty creatures to prey upon it and corrupt it. The current wave
of rape incidents in regions where public exposure prevails, as
well as in the widening phenomenon of infidelity, strengthens
our argument beyond any doubt. p. 36.

Are men going to put up with being called "swarms of dirty creatures?"
Can we allow the idea to persist that you have no self-control when you see
an attractive, unmasked woman? Every time I read the above statement I was
amused at the phrasing but outraged at the imagery. From a man in a culture

where men may have multiple spouses but women may have only one, the reader can deduct whose infidelity they are talking about.

Shortly after I arrived, an old friend from home wrote the following to me:

Do you know why Moslims (sp) wear veils?

Tamerlane had a favorite wife and while he was off fighting, she decided to build a mosque in his honor. However, the architect fell in love with her and slowed things down, so he could be with her longer. One day, when it was finally built, he asked if he may kiss her. She said, yes, thru her hand. So she put her hand on her cheek and he kissed her hand. The ardor went clear thru and left a mark on her face. Tamerlane was delighted with the mosque, but when he saw her face, he was very angry and decreed that from then on, all women should be veiled. This mosque is in Samarkand and is being restored. (The latter is no fairy tale.)

Others in Saudi Arabia blamed it on the Turks. Saudis are prone to blame many things on their ancient enemies, the Turks. When the Turks under Ataturk modernized and discarded the veil, the Saudis took this custom and gave it permanency. Some have tried to blame this cruel custom on the Bedouin, but the country Bedouin I saw did not veil their women until they came into the city. The modern Saudis had taken that phrase from the Koran 'Draw their veils over their bosoms . . .'' and misconstrued it to convince modern Saudi women to immure themselves behind their veils and behind their walls.

Egyptian friends said that their imams, religious leaders, required that only their head and neck be covered. The nationality of the women could often be identified by the amount of their body left uncovered. Covering the head and neck did not keep them from being objects of attention. Men invariably looked at an uncovered face. Faces that would have drawn no attention in the West, attracted stares in Saudi Arabia.

On several occasions, I found it expedient to wear the veil when I accompanied students. This involved first wrapping a piece of black cotton gauze of double thickness around my face. Then a scarf of silk or rayon was put around over my hair. Then the abaya was drawn up over the back of my head and I clutched it in front. Somehow, the Saudi women managed not to need to clutch it like I did. While with other women, the black gauze could be brought up and folded back over the silk scarf to reveal the face until such a moment when veiling was required if a man appeared. Each time I dressed thusly, the Saudi women and students who saw me complimented me on how beautiful I looked. I thought I looked ghastly, but somehow, they thought it looked beautiful. This feeling they expressed was confirmed when babies cried at my unveiled face, but just observed me with the same curiosity they observed all adults when my face or even just my hair was covered. Maybe it was the red hair that was the threat. The quality of the red henna in Saudi Arabia was just too tempting to bypass.

I was fascinated to observe in the hospital how children unfailingly found their own mothers, despite the fact that they all looked alike when veiled. Upon several occasions I had the opportunity to sit in the women's waiting corridor at the hospital during clinic hours. The women would squat in a row along the corridor wall, one black figure after another along the entire twenty yard length of the hallway. It was necessary to be veiled since men doctors, x-ray technicians and husbands walked up and down the hall. The children would play on the square of grass in front of the hospital coming in at intervals to check on the continuing presence of their mothers. As the women advanced toward their turn with the doctor, their position against the wall changed. The children would come running in down between the black squatting figures and not infrequently run up to the wrong person. The woman would say something to indicate that she was not the one. The child would look around and invariably, on the second try, go straight to their mother. Maybe the child recognized her feet or her smell, but to me, the Saudis were remarkably odor free for the climate in which they lived.

In the booklet *Teaching at the University of Riyadh* given to me at the Consular Office of Houston, it gave the following advice regarding clothing:

> For women: In the city street, foreign women are most conformable in long skirts and long sleeves with conservative colors. Sleeveless dress, low cut necklines, shorts or miniskirts are not tolerated since Moslem law requires women to be dressed in modesty. Around the house, shirtwaist dresses, blouses, skirts and pants with tunics can be worn. You may want to bring along with you some long dresses for evening wear. And if you sew, you will want to bring your sewing machine.

Well, this last bit of advice was the best. I did bring along my Singer sewing machine. It arrived by air freight three weeks after my arrival. I used it frequently to make up for lacks in my own wardrobe as well as mending for many other foreigners. Between the time the booklet was printed and the time I arrived, the traditionalists attempted to take over the Grand Mosque in Mecca in November 1979. In order to salve the Saudis who supported that conservatism, the University came out with more conservative dress codes for both students and teachers. When I arrived, posters with the required type dress were plastered all over the campus. Fortunately for me, I had talked by long-distance telephone with a woman who had already spent a year at the University. She was able to advise me to bring a few more long things as they were required at all times, not just for evenings and in the street. This particular chronology of events points up the fact that during my residence, the dress code became progressively stricter. My three long skirts from "hippy" California had to be quickly supplemented with others I made as well as some I bought in the *hareem* or women's souq.

By the middle of my first year, the American government was advising American women to cover their heads upon leaving their compounds. During my second year, I began to hear frequent stories of women being arrested for wearing blue-jeans in supermarkets and public chastisements for "improper dress". In early March 1982, there appeared in the supermarkets the following:

IMPORTANT NOTICE

In accordance with official orders and regulations currently in force, all expatriates coming to his country, whether muslims or non-muslims, are requested to abide by the regulations and customs of the country. It is, therefore, expressly forbidden for women to go out without covering their heads and limbs. Fines will be imposed on those breaking these regulations.

Thank you for your understanding and cooperation.

God's mercy and blessings be with you.

The newsletter of one of the US government groups thoughtfully published this notice for distribution in its regular publication, but none of the places of employment where there were big concentrations of multi-national women such as in the University or in the various hospitals were given this warning. We were left to learn it the hard way. I am grateful that my American government took this kind of care of its employees.

Personally, I knew of three friends who had mutawahs try to enforce this new regulation in addition to my own final episode. In a main supermarket, a US educated Jordanian had the mutawah approach him and tell him to have his wife, who was visiting from Amman, cover her head and wear long dresses. In a different supermarket, an American government employee was taken into custody by two mutawahs the moment his beautiful wife left his side to go off shopping in another aisle. He had a difficult time as they tried to appropriate his Official American Passport and his Saudi divers' license. He played "dumb" and got free from them, grabbed his wife and fled. The third incident involved the daughter of one of my Egyptian colleagues. Her husband was taking the eight-year-old girl to visit a bookstore on the main street. A mutawah followed the father and daughter into the store and admonished the father to have his daughter wear long sleeves. She was already wearing a long dress. The child was amused by the incident and began to laugh. Her father had to caution her to be quiet, lest he get more trouble from the mutawah. When I met this family on the street, a few days later, the eight-year-old was 'properly sleeved'.

On my last night in Riyadh, I was so excited about my anticipated departure that I forgot and went to the souq with my head uncovered. I, who had begun to cover my head long before other Western women did, became careless. Perhaps it was because I was in the company of two American Army Colonels carrying prestigious identification of the Saudi National Guard that I relaxed my guard and neglected my usual care in abiding by the rigid rules. On our first stroll through the women's clothing souq, no one seemed to pay attention to my uncovered red hair. But on our return trip, as we entered the main alley of the women's souq, the old bearded mutawah brought his wooden stave down sharply in front of me. He said to me in Arabic "Where is your head cover?" Fortunately for me, I had not dropped my guard entirely. I quickly pulled a black scarf out of my purse and slipped it over my hair. The old man lowered the stick and we were allowed to proceed. A Muslim friend later told me that I had barely missed arrest on my last night in Saudi Arabia since it was the beginning of Ramadan, the fasting time when tempers are short. My companion' Saudi National Guard identification cards probably would have kept us all out of jail, but it would not have been good to spend my last night in the police station. And the fact that I was with two men to whom I was not married had more potential for trouble. I was lucky!

Men were not neglected in the advice given in the University booklet:

> For Men: Open-necked short sleeved shirts and light weight trousers are worn with sweaters and casual jackets for cool weather. Light weight suits can be useful in Riyadh. Men do not wear short pants.

This last injunction was enforced as well. A man I knew was out in jogging shorts. In my journal I recorded an incident that happened to him:

> A van of mutawahs came along behind him in the street and called "STOP" in English three times, which he ignored since mutawahs don't have uniforms and look like everyone else. So they drove the van up unto the sidewalk and blocked his path. They told him if they ever caught him out again without both legs and arms completely covered, they would take him straight to jail without further discussion.

Generally there was more variety in men's public dress than there was in women's. Women almost all wore long sleeved long dresses in public, except Pakistanis who wore their traditional Pakistani suits with baggy pants. The Sudanese women wore street length dresses covered by a cloth two yards wide and about five yards long which they constantly adjusted to keep themselves adequately covered to meet Saudi standards. The Ethiopians and Eritreans used the same style but with a white cloth. This seemed the best choice for that "oven" climate.

The variety in men's dress included the Saudi traditional *thobe, ghutra* and *igal*. The *thobe* is the long robe which is used with many variations throughout the Middle East. In Saudi Arabia, the neck and shoulders look like the white Western dress shirt except it doesn't stop midway but continues on down to the floor. It has just as many variational frills as Western shirts; French cuffs, tucks, bibs, ruffles, gold stud buttons, etc. Apparently, the richer and more important the man, the more embellishments, but I acknowledge that this assumption is not always true in either culture. In winter, there were some extremely handsome tailored sets of *thobe*, matching vest and jacket. I always wondered if the wearer were a prince, a *sheik* or a pretender.

The *ghutra* is the cloth with which they covered their heads. In Saudi Arabia, it was usually white with red embroidery and easily simulated with a red-checkered table cloth for the Wise Men in Christmas plays. Business and professional men frequently used white ones, some embellished with beautiful white embroidery. The various nationalities had typical colors for their *ghutras*. Yemenis used green with bright colored tassels. This was my favorite. Iraqis used black and white while Egyptians used brown, but they were not always consistent in this so it could not be used as an accurate method of identifying nationalities. The Sudanese and other Africans used the long head cloth which they wound turban-style around their heads. These long clothes could be dangerous. One Sudanese man I knew had his turban come unwrapped while he was driving. The end caught in the back left wheel and jerked his head back giving him a good case of "whiplash". The adage from the author is "Draping clothes and machinery don't mix." Just try draping a card table cloth over your head and driving your car, for example.

The *igal* is the set of black rings worn over the *ghutra* to hold it down and supposedly was originally used as a camel hobble. The Saudis and other Peninsula Arabs, with the exception of the Yemenis, usually wear *igals*. Westerners frequently called the *igal* "the fan-belt" since it is about the same size and appearance. It is a rope wrapped with black yarn. It is twisted and doubled before being pulled down over the *ghutra* which itself is pulled over a small white embroidered skullcap, similar to the Jewish "yarmulke".

Of all the costumes, the most colorful were the Yemenis. They usually did not wear the *igal*. They just wrapped the *ghutra* they had almost any old way that suited the weather; across the face in a dust storm, around the neck in cold weather, or wrapped like a sweat band in hot weather. They wore a regular shirt usually of some bright color or plaid. To cover their lower limbs, they wore a skirt. It was a kind of haphazard affair, two yards of cloth temporarily pleated and held in place by an embroidered belt. At home in their own land, or out in the desert, the belt also held a sheathed knife or gun. I felt the Yemenis were the most charming of all the Middle Easterners, in personality as well as dress. They lacked the affectations and defensiveness I perceived in other Arabs. The wonderfully crafted silver jewelry worn all over the Peninsula by the Bedouin was usually of Yemeni manufacture.

Some Egyptian men and women both wore their national dress, the *galabaya*, a loose fitting robe decorated with braid or embroidery for women or plain for men. Many of the men also wore a turban. Generally, Egyptian men were indistinguishable from Western men in their sport-shirts or business suits. For women, the *galabaya* met all the standard requirements put forth by the Saudis so most Egyptian women found it to be convenient to wear their national dress.

The *ihram* dress is the costume worn by those making a pilgrimage or *umra*, a lesser pilgrimage. There are different requirements for men and women as there are for most things in Saudi society, though the pilgrimage laws include all Muslims. Both sexes are encouraged to bath and perfume themselves as the *miqqat*, a dressing station at the entrance to the pilgrimage grounds. Men then don two white seamless lengths of cloth, one around the torso and over one shoulder while the other goes around the hips. Pilgrimage clothing for women is less rigidly specified, except that it be unalluring and there should be no seams in her veil or gloves. The *ihram* veil is not used to cover the face. Professor Al Omar (1975) says women can veil their faces "if she finds herself surrounded by men". My female Muslim friends were emphatic that there should be no face covering during wearing of the *ihram* costume. These two ideas represent to me, the conflicts arising from the evolution of women toward more self-mastery.

After assumption of the ihram dressing, it is forbidden to kiss, have sex-relations, propose marriage, remove body hair, clip finger or toenails, apply or smell perfume, or kill game animals. Men may not cover their heads except by an umbrella or tent shadow. Neither may they wear shoes, only sandals.

Clothing was in transition as the Saudis tried to decide what from the old tradition should be incorporated with their new image as world financiers.

REFERENCES:

Abdul-Rauf, Muhammad (1973). *The Islamic View of Women*. NY: Robert Speller & Sons, Publisher, Inc.

Ali, Abdallah Yousef (1931) *The Quran*. Egypt.

Al-Omar, Professor Abdul Rahman Ben (1975) *Islam the Religion of Truth*. Kingdom of Saudi Arabia: The Supreme Head Office for Religious Researches, Ifta, Call, and Guidance Departments.

Beck, Lois & Keddie, Nikki (1978) *Women in the Muslim World*. Cambridge, MA: Harvard University Press.

Cirlot, J. E. (1962). *A Dictionary of Symbols*. London: Routledge & Kegan Paul Ltd.

SHELTER

Muslims and Saudis in particular are very concerned with privacy.

Introduction to Section 4 Sura XXIV
Privacy in the home is a nurse of virtue:
Respect it with dignity and decorum. Guard
Your eyes and thoughts with rules of modesty
In dress and manners: and learn from these
To keep your spiritual gaze from straying
To any but God. True marriage should teach
Us chastity and purity, and such
Are the virtues which lead us to the Light
Sublime which illuminates the world.

Verse 27
Ye who believe!
Enter not other houses than
Your own, until ye have
Asked permission and saluted
Those in them: that is
Best for you, in order that
Ye may heed (what is seemly).

Verse 28
If ye find no one
In the house, enter not
Until permission is given
To you: if ye are asked
To go back, go back:
That makes for greater purity
For yourselves: and God
Knows well all that ye do.

In looking at Saudi Arabia today, the following passage points up the continuity of their traditions with present attitudes:

Sura XVI Verse 80
It is God who made your habitations
Homes of rest and quiet
For you: and made for you,
Out of the skins of animals,
(Tents for) dwellings, which
Ye find so light (and handy)
When ye travel and when
Ye stop (in your travels);
And out of their wool,
And their soft fibers
(Between wool and hair),
And their hair, rich stuff
And articles of convenience
(To serve you) for a time.

Whenever dignitaries came whom they wanted to impress with Arabian culture, they were taken to a special hospitality tent set up on the outskirts of the city. Bedouin tents, open in front, have a quality of invitation which portrays hospitality but also requires the guest to remember the injunction of the Koran about observing privacy. Because privacy is so hard to come by in a flat land, they must exert their minds to devise privacy where it does not exist. People on the outside of tents, can usually hear everything that happens on the inside of tents, unless a conscious effort is made to ignore it.

Authentic Bedouin tents have a dividing curtain to demarcate the women's section from the men's. The men's section was frequently open for all to see the meager furnishings, the coffee making equipment, the brazier, the painted trunks, cushions and carpets. On occasion, out away from the city, I was able to see inside the women's section. It looked similar to the men's but without the coffee equipment. There are much better sources for details on Bedouin life than I am able to provide in the reference list. And with each year, their numbers increase. One researcher Dr. Zohair A. Sebai (1981) states, "The estimated proportion of nomads decreased from thirty percent in 1967 to less than twenty percent in 1981." Soon, perhaps, the black woolen Bedouin tents will be seen only in museums, though they were still a common sight when we left the metropolitan areas. In fact, when I visited Hafar Al Batin near the Iraqi border in October 1981, nearly one half of the habitations in that small city were the lovely black Bedouin tents. Perhaps they will retain the tents while giving up the life that required them, as we did with out log cabins.

Riyadh is not typical of Saudi Arabia. It is the capital city. Capital cities always have the national flavor a little diluted by all the other nationalities and the things done to cater to their need and wants. Since it is the main place in which I entered homes, I must describe it no matter how dilute.

I learned the difference between flats and apartments soon after arrival, a distinction I'd never been required to make before. Flats are cheap and apartments are expensive. Flats are what common people live in and apartments are for the wealthy who do not want to live in a house. I was provided a "flat" by the University.

Most villas, as well as flats and apartments were divided into easily recognizable "women's" sections and "men's" sections. The men's section was near the front door or central reception hall so that when male visitors arrived, they had no need to pass through the women's domain. Even American government villas rented for USA employees had a similar plan. Several American men told of being invited to Saudi homes for dinner. They were seated in the front room and never saw anything beyond that room. The men brought in the food which had been prepared by the women in the back. They reported the strange sensation of being aware of the presence of women nearby, but never having any proof. There was no discussion or acknowledgement of their presence or existence.

Women were assumed to be unable to live alone, for a variety of reasons, the foremost of which is that they were expected to be so weak willed that they would not be able to abide by moral codes, the religious codes of Islam, without a chaperone. If they had another women present, it was thought to be some sort of curb on their natural erotic inclinations. These were not assumptions. Saudi men stated exactly those ideas in my presence. Therefore, I was required to live with a flat-mate during most of my residence. That was a hard thing for a grown American woman to do, but I did it for two years.

The first flat in which I lived was built by a German construction company and was as precise as could be wanted. It had central heating and air-conditioning. The floors were covered with plain gray felt of a thickness of one quarter of an inch. It was perfect for showing off the lovely 'oriental' carpets available in the souq. Windows to the outside were scarce. Centuries of looking out on nothing but sand may have made them not feel the need for windows, because they surely did not have many. On the ground floor, even those they did have had were usually frosted glass. My second flat was on the ground floor, so I always felt a little like I was living in a cave. Most windows and balconies had some sort of blind, not inside where it was adjustable, but outside where it could not be moved easily. This meant that even flats which should have had a view had it blocked by a metal lattice or frosted glass panel set away from the wall so air could enter but eyes could not. They were so rigorous about barring eyes from their private areas. At the University, we had four balconies on our building, but these balconies all had walls at least six feet high. The only way to see over was to pull a chair out unto the balcony and stand on it, which I did on many occasions to look for the bus or to see if my favorite sandwich shop had closed for prayer.

Many of the screens on the windows were so ill-fitting that it gave easy access to those female mosquitoes looking for warm blood to hatch their eggs from January through May. Only when it was fiercely hot and I no longer to open my windows was it safe to do so. The wall around my bed was speckled with my own blood given up when I squashed my small enemies. Fortunately, malaria was not a hazard in the Central Desert as it was on the Coast.

There were enormous blocks of flats being started and finished regularly. I wondered, when almost one third of their 1981 residents were expatriates, what they planned to do with all those flats, after the foreigners go home. But at their rapid birthrate, perhaps they will fill them themselves in twenty years. Never mind how they intend to use them; they are being built to heights of twenty stories. When I arrived, the common joke was "Do you know what the national bird of Saudi Arabia is?" Answer! "The crane" because there were so many building cranes silhouetted against the sky. They seemed also to have few qualms about knocking down existing buildings, some as young as twenty years or less. They were also demolishing many of the old mud sections of the city. Some through which I walked the first year, were construction sites for flats during my second year. When Dr. Al-Masry, Minister of Antiquities was asked about this, he responded, "The people who complain about tearing down the old mud houses would not be willing to live there." It was interesting to walk through these old sections where the alleys were sometimes so narrow, only a skinny "unloaded" camel could make his way down them. And it was not so long ago, that the alleys had open sewers running down the middle. On occasion, I still saw open sewers. There was a five hundred year old village about nine miles from Riyadh. Part of it was in ruins from the time of war with the Ottoman Empire, but the remainder was still in use. They decorated the interiors with primitive molded plaster in geometric designs, some having great complexity. Upper rooms had columns making a balcony, just like the drawings from my childhood *Bible* story picture books.

"Villa" was the term used to refer to what we would call a house. Most were entered through a central hall, the sort found in our Victorian houses, with receiving rooms off to the sides. It was difficult to determine what the designers had had in mind for the different rooms as they were all alike, without closets; with doors opening off the central hallway. Only some villas in the American compounds I visited seemed to be designed with the purpose of the individual rooms in mind. Villas usually had some courtyard either between the front gate and the door or in the middle of the building as in Mexico. The walls around the villas were usually twelve to fourteen feet high, for the usual reason, privacy and to guard women against forbidden eyes. While these high walls provided some shade, except at mid-day, they effectively blocked any breeze.

The bathrooms were enormous, covered from floor to ceiling in lively tile. Only luxury homes had such bathrooms in the USA in 1982. Each home I was in had at least one bidet. I promised myself that someday, I would have one in my California home. They were so convenient, once I got used to them. Usually a second bathroom had an "Eastern" toilet, which was a special sort of sink in the floor, usually with raised spots to put feet while squatting over the hole. Never mind how healthy it is supposed to be for the intestinal track to defecate squatting, I felt I could never get used to them. My first experience trying to use one was during my first week when the University required me to have a urine test. They handed me a specimen bottle and indicated a door across the hospital corridor. I had to step up about fourteen inches into a tiny room in which I could hardly stand up and turn around. In the floor was the "Eastern" toilet, the first I had seen. I had to hold up my long skirt, which I wasn't used to, squat and aim for the bottle all at once, no mean feat! My lack of success did not encourage me to want to use them on a regular basis.

The furniture arrangement of the typical Arab house, even those of middle class professionals, was that one or two rooms would be furnished with upholstered Western style furniture. The other rooms were furnished with carpets and the walls lined with cushions. The cushions were usually about five inches thick and fourteen inches high, upholstered in some loud brocade and completely lining the wall of the room near the floor and on the floor itself. About every four feet, there would be an arm rest type cushion sticking out into the room something for a person to rest against while sitting on the floor cushions. Pictures were usually hung too high to look at without craning one's neck. Most wall decorations had an Islamic message or overtone. They might be pictures of Mecca during the pilgrimage prayers or brass letters stating one of the favorite Koranic verses. Saudi kitchens had very little table or counter space. They did much of their work of food preparation on the floor. Despite the fact that they do limit their physical activity, I must note that they do keep themselves limber enough to get up and down to the floor throughout their lives. Think about American grandparents. Can they do that into their seventies? Maybe praying and touching their heads to the floor five times per day has these worthy effects.

The souqs which provided the furnishings were perennially interesting to me. The carpet souq was in a dim alley lined on either side with six yard by six yard shops which were stacked from floor to ceiling with all the rich variety of carpets from throughout the East and Middle East. Bedouin men stood in the middle of the alley with carpets spread before them that they were trying to sell to the souq vendors. It had all the hurley-burley and hustle-bustle exotic flavor I associated with caravan routes, the Kasbah, spy movies and Lawrence of Arabia. I weakened the strings on my purse often in that seductive place. The souq vendors began to know me. On one occasion during my first year, I went one evening with a friend and no money as I had learned to do to protect my purse because of my weakness for the luscious colors and designs, when one of the vendors saw me admiring a dirty and rough but interesting old Bedouin carpet. He vowed it was authentic Saudi Arabian. When he offered it to me at a low price, I gave my protective response, "No Money!" He said "OK, never mind, you take the carpet and bring me the five hundred riyals tomorrow or the day after." No paper signing, nothing! But I did not want to clean that old carpet even though it was only one hundred fifty dollars.

In the rooms furnished ala Western style, there were usually massive overstuffed chairs and sofas with chrome frames which were pushed back against the walls making the room look like an audience hall and not inclining me to conversation. Depending upon the taste, some overstuffed furniture frames were beautifully carved hardwood. These rooms were the ones in which they held the "ladies parties" which I attended. There would be small square tables placed in front of and between sofas and chairs. On the tables would be ornate brocade doilies and boxes of Kleenex. These Western rooms were used on special occasions and otherwise seldom used by the family. Stores which sold these Western furnishings reminded me of the term "nouveau riche" which conjured up visions of vast quantities of money and no preparation for making decisions about spending it. This attitude was probably true of the culture in general. Only a few decades away from the Spartan Bedouin life, they had little background for discriminating the gaudy from the glossy from the good.

I was never able to visit a real "palace" while it was being lived in by a real prince, princess, sheik or sheikess. My only opportunity to see the inside was the palace where our college dean had his office. It had been stripped of its elegant furnishings by then. The remnants of its former splendor were the watermark patterned taffeta wall covers and the elaborate purple bathrooms with gold plated faucets and hardware. Though it was called "The Palace" it did not seem palatial to me, lacking the grandeur I associate with the word. However, I occasionally got glimpses in through the guarded doors into palatial courtyards. I could see through the latticed gates into the courtyards of the palaces of King Khalid, Crown Prince Fahad, Prince Talal and Prince Abdullah. Usually there were enough splendiferous hanging lamps and window screens outside that I could imagine what the inside would hold. Sometimes, I would have strong feelings of re-viewing scenes from my childhood book of the *Arabian Nights*. One of the most amusing palaces was a copy of the USA White House. Rumors flew about who really owned it, as well as the story that after completion, it had been gutted and rebuilt because the Pakistani contractor who reportedly built it, had used such shoddy materials and techniques that is was falling apart before it was lived in. That story was not hard to believe because I could see the wretched building procedures, even to a laywoman's eyes while waiting for the bus. Bricks were not aligned. Mortar was made by making a hole in the middle of a pile of sand on the sidewalk and just pouring in water and cement and using the outside of the pile of sand as the mixing bowl. Plumbing looked as if it were installed as an afterthought with pipes running up the sides of otherwise lovely buildings. Despite this entire negative report, Riyadh does have some of the most interesting, attractive and varied big buildings I had ever seen. I predicted that when it was finished, the city would truly portray the splendors of the *Arabian Nights*.

On one occasion, I was able to join a tour of the Murraba Palace, former residence of Kind Ibn Saud, the unifier of modern Arabia. Interestingly, historical sites like this old palace built in the 1930s, are not open to the public, only to special tours arranged with difficulty through the Department of Antiquities. In its time, that palace was probably about as splendid as possible. It was a two story mud structure with rooms on both floors entirely surrounding the stone flagged courtyard. Both floors had a roofed walkway around the inside of the courtyard and all rooms gave out unto this portico. The King's audience hall was just as it had been when he used it forty years ago. Blue brocade upholstered and carved chairs lined the walls and were arranged in rows between the columns that were holding up the center of the room. The windows were all slightly skewed, with apparently no line level with the compass. It had its own charm but also reminded me of how little progress had been made in some construction from the extremely primitive techniques apparent there. As I stood in the interior court waiting for the other members of the tour to finish, I had a fantasy that I was present at a feast held there on the flagstones. I was seated on a brightly colored carpet, eating roast camel with my right hand and wiping grease off my chin with my left.

REFERENCES:

Ali, Abdallah Yousef (1931) *The Quran*. Egypt.

Sebai, Zohair A. (1981). *The Health of the Family in a Changing Arabia*. Jeddah, Saudi Arabia: Tihama Publications.

6

WOMEN & SEX

Sura IV Verse 1
And (reverence) the wombs
(That bore you); for God
Ever watches over you.

There is a lot written in the Koran about women. It seems to cover the main points in reference to women and sex; birth, marriage, divorce, widowhood, rights, and chastity.

Sura II Verse 20
The society must live under laws.
Marriage, divorce, and widowhood
To be regulated; and the rights of women,
Apt to be trampled underfoot,
Now clearly affirmed.

Nowhere does it seem to say that men and women should be kept separate. The Saudi preoccupation with the separation of the sexes probably had its roots buried in tribal custom. It was easier to protect property collected in one place than spread about. Nomads who were vulnerable to surprise attack upon every occasion, might more easily have protected their female property if they were together hidden away from the men, the visible warriors. The enemy might not guess their vulnerability if the women were not seen. Women can't impregnate women while backs are turned, but men can and will.

Introduction to Sura 55
Let not believing women
Be handed over to Unbelievers:
No marriage tie is lawful between them.
When women wish to join your society
Take their assurance that they yield not
To sin or unbeseeming conduct.
Take every care to keep your society
Free and pure, and self-contained.

The idea expressed in this introduction is the basis for the policy of not allowing women to leave the country without an accompanying male relative. Young women who have left Saudi Arabia to study have "fallen in love" with Unbelievers, an impossible match by Saudi standards. Men can marry outside the country and outside the religion, but not the Saudi women.

Introduction to Sura 65
Guard well your truth and pure integrity
In sex relations. Keep the tie
Of marriage sacred; but where it must
Be dissolved, use all precautions to ensure
Justice to the weaker party and protect
The interests of the unborn or newborn lives
As well as social decency; close not
To the last the door of reconciliation.

Introduction to Sura 66
The relations between the sexes are embittered
By misunderstandings and conflicts that produce
Unhappiness and misery, personal and social.
Harmony and confidence are due between
The sexes, not disgust or isolation, which may
Please some but cause injustice to others.
Respect each other's confidence, and if
You fail, repent and make amends.
The good man seeks virtue for himself
And his family.

In one of my early diary entries, I referred to Saudi Arabia as "this sexually enigmatic place". The dictionary definition of enigmatic as "obscure, ambiguous, darkly expressed, anything such as a motive for conduct which is inexplicable to the observer". The Koranic writings were not enigmatic to me. I could understand them. But Saudi Arabia continued to be an enigma to me even after two years.

W. Montgomery Watt (1961) gave a few clues about this culture/religious preoccupation with keeping women subservient, out of any position where power is a function; for example, women are forbidden to hold driver's licenses and consequently forbidden to drive in Saudi Arabia, as well as to hold top positions in organizations. Though Watt says the "evidence is scanty" he alludes in three different following passages to the probability that Saudi society at the time of the Prophet Mohamed was changing both familially and religiously from matrilineal to patralineal and from matriarchy to patriarchy:

> . . . there may have been a change from a matrilineal system to a patralineal one. . . . these cases of confederacy may have been introduced by the Islamic authors of records to explain group cohesion on the matrilineal basis that was inexplicable on their own patralineal principles.

A man called Ka'b ibn-al-Ashraf, prominent as a poet and an opponent of Muhammad, was the son of an Arab man (either pagan or, more probably, Christian) and a Jewish woman: but he was recorded as belonging to his mother's clan of al-Nadir. The insistence of Ka'b ibn-al-Ashraf suggests that they (Jews) had adopted some Arab marriage practices (such as uxorilocal marriage) and a measure of matrilineal kinship.

These excerpts from *Islam and the Integration of Society* allude to the probable emergence of Mohamed the Prophet from the upheaval resulting from the change from matriarchy to patriarchy among the Semites. Since the fertility goddesses of matriarchies were commonly believed to be "idolatrous" statues, this theory would fit with the Prophet's rampage against "idols". It could explain somewhat the heavy repression of women in Islam. If the religion was born at a time when the culture felt the need to root out pagan femaleness, the impact of this excoriation during the development may have been buried in the cultural unconscious in much the same way as an individual buries traumatic events of the growth years. Hence now, this treatment could be taken as "revelation" along with the rest of the Islamic tradition.

This repression was cloaked in the Saudi strict "separation of the sexes." It was the same as our "separate but equal" tradition practiced before the civil rights movement. An example of how it worked, was whenever they had an exhibit or special show such as at the zoo, the museum or a book faire, there were special days for women, usually less than one third of the time the show was open. In order to attend, a woman had to have someone chauffeur her. She had to know how to go to the place of exhibition in order to direct the driver. Since she was not allowed to drive, it was difficult for her to learn the routes. Once as the exhibition, she had to ask the driver to wait in the hot sun for her while she was ushered into the guarded precincts. This situation discouraged many women from attending even those events at which their presence was allowed. In this way, they were subtly denied knowledge, experience and awareness of new developments. If knowledge is power as we are frequently told in the West, they were kept deviously weak, for they were told it was for their own protection. They were told that men were unable to control themselves; therefore, they must be kept separate.

There were two Arabic words which pretty much controlled a woman's male associates. *Maharram* means the males with whom it is all right for a woman to be alone, men she cannot marry or remarry; father uncle, brother, son or father. The second word is *sohbah*, or safe company. The literal meaning is "good company" protective company but not *maharram*. An employer could be a *sohbah*. When two of us women teachers took three students to another city for clinical practice in a specialty hospital, a *sohbah* or administrative assistant was sent with us, the assumption being that we required male supervision, despite the fact that our specialized professional knowledge was felt to be necessary and otherwise unavailable in the Kingdom.

The Saudis seemed not to draw the relationship between how one treated others and whether those others wanted to remain close. Traditionally, all close ties were family oriented. No matter what a person did, if he or she was in the family, they were the family's responsibility. From this traditional base, men had the right and responsibility to protect their family from shame by chastising their women. Women had no alternatives, no other place to go so they accepted whatever treatment the family dealt out. However, things changed and Saudis began dealing with many Western and non-Muslim women. They had not yet learned to see the cause and effect relationship between their treatment of the woman and her willingness to re-contract with them. This caused frequent problems. Eventually, if they learn this cause and effect lesson, I predict that Saudi women will be the beneficiaries. However, since that tradition is the "revealed" word of God, it may be a long time a-coming.

Sura IV Introduction to Section 6
Men are the protectors

And maintainers of women,
Because God has given
The one more (strength)
Than the other, and because
They support them from their means.
Therefore the righteous woman
Are devoutly obedient, and guard
In (the husband's) absence
What God would have them guard.
As to those women
On whose part ye fear
Disloyalty and ill-conduct,
Admonish them (first),
(Next), refuse to share their beds,
(And last) beat them (lightly);
But if they return to obedience,
Seek not against them
Means (of annoyance):

The Prophet's attempt to simulate equality obviously failed, by our Western standards. Current writers in 1982 attempted the same thing such as the one titled "Women and Islam" in the *Arab News*, the biggest English language daily newspaper in the Kingdom.

> That Islam also makes man superior does not mean that women suffer any degree of injustice under Islam. Indeed, the reverse is true. For just as Islam recognizes man's superiority, it does not approve subjugation of women. It provides a social and family system which assigns to each of the two sexes its proper human position and which enables them both to make their proper contributions to the advancement of mankind.
>
> ....Today we intend to look very briefly at the main position in its overall concept of human life. First, Islam considers that together men and women constitute the human race. Hence, they share equally in its main qualities. There is no denial of the fact that women share equally with men the responsibility of the preservation of humanity. . . .
>
> Second, unlike other religions, Islam does not lay the blame in man's fall from heaven on women alone. Every time Adam's story is referred to in the Qur'an the sin which led to the fall is stated to have been committed by both Adam and Eve. . . .

Finally, Islam assigns the patronage over women to their immediate relatives and makes those relatives answerable for taking good care of their women. It, however, gives women equal rights to own property and dispose of it by any contractual dealings without any restrictions whatsoever, apart from those that apply to all Islamic dealings.

. . . one wonders why Islam is constantly accused of being unfair to women.

My mother's favorite adage, "Actions speak louder than words" is the best answer I can give to Mr. Salahi. When women have no mobility without men, no decision making power over their children, it is difficult to take his protestation seriously. When this series of five articles appeared, it set the University English speaking teachers abuzz. The articles were photocopied and shared. Outrage was the predominant emotion expressed by these Western women. We knew that these hypocrisies existed, as we experienced them daily, but to see them in print scratched a raw nerve.

The Saudi attempt to carry out complete separation of the sexes had more success than failure. In education at all levels above kindergarten, boys were taught by men and girls were taught by women. Women's schooling usually took place behind fourteen foot walls, ostensibly to assure that no men would see them. If I saw a fourteen foot wall there was a good chance female education occurred behind it. Boys' schools generally had only six foot walls. Even special education for the deaf, blind and mentally retarded was separate. Economically, it meant there were costly separate systems and services such as libraries, administration offices, waiting rooms, campuses, and cafeterias. This was an extravagance most Western countries would probably never again choose. I wondered if the Saudis again found themselves a poor desert country, would economics force them to combine male and female education to save money. Or would the efforts to educate women cease? Female education has made most of its advances since the glut of oil dollars. This is a coincidence according to Beck and Keddie (1978):

There is a possibility that economic development could affect women's educational achievement, but statistical tests reveal little relationship among per capita gross national product, restrictiveness, and women's education. Relatively poor Muslim states, such as Turkey and Tunisia have reformed many laws affecting women and encouraging female education, while some wealthier countries, such as Libya and Saudi Arabia, have introduced few or no reforms and report low educational achievement of women. p. 20

Saudi University education, of course, was carefully segregated for students as well as staff. No men were allowed unto campus for any purpose until after eight at night when the iron doors between the girls' hostel, the dormitory which was called the "jail" by the students and the campus class buildings were locked, or on school holidays when the campus was also locked to students.

This campus first had female students in 1970. After 10 am on a school day, I would see big bunches of men waiting outside the main gate to drive their female relatives home from school, that is any relatives except cousins. Since cousins are marriageable, consorting was not allowed. An entry in my diary describes the gate scene as follows;

> "There is a little booth outside the gate. It has a little shelf about twenty four inches off the ground with a roof over it. The guard can squat on the shelf and keep out of the sun, while he makes sure that no men see inside the gate. Half of the time the guard is not in evidence. There is a microphone on a hook by his booth. He is supposed to announce the name of the student for whom some man is waiting, but usually he just hands the microphone to the man to call his own female relative. So as one approaches the corner of the campus, names of various students can be heard as they are called over the loudspeaker. Just inside the gate there is another twelve foot high metal barrier so that even if a man looks in the door, he sees only a blank wall unless one of the girls is looking out, but of course, she covers her face with black gauze before peeking around the gate. In the corridor near the gate between two buildings, chairs with writing arms line both sides so students can sit and study while they wait for their rides. But they just sit and visit until their name is called."

The above scene included only residents of Riyadh, since all non-Riyadh residents lived in the closely guarded adjacent hostel. During my first year, I had met the entire family of one of my students. During the second year, they came from Mecca to visit her and she promised to bring them to visit me. They did not arrive. The following Saturday which is like Monday in the USA, the first day of the school week, she came and told me that her brother had only his passport and not the proper kinship proof paper from the government, he had not been allowed to bring her to my flat. In fact, he had not even been allowed to see her under they eyes of the male guard. She had not been aware of this new requirement for kinship proof beyond the passport. She was so angry; she retaliated by keeping her sister in the hostel overnight which was forbidden. I thought up the following adage: "Repression causes subversion" based upon the above situation.

The girls' hostel was the equivalent of our campus dormitories, except it was enclosed inside the fourteen foot walls and adjoined the campus proper. It had basketball and volleyball courts, a swimming pool which had no plumbing or drainage. It was necessary to fill and drain it with hoses from the top. The bottom was covered with old soda cans and waste paper. I wondered how it could have been allowed to be built without plumbing.

The exit/entrance to the hostel was even more closely guarded than the campus. Each time I entered from the street, the guards challenged my right to enter. Once I was even stopped at the check point by the door between the hostel and the campus, where resident students produced and turned in an identification card which they retrieved when they returned. This was to assure that no students would leave the campus with anyone, since her unretrieved card would call the alarm. This safeguard had come about after a student had been discovered slipping off by the campus gate to be with her boyfriend. Because I had a friend whose faculty office was within the hostel confines, I was allowed entrance. Female teachers, who could name no destination within, would not be allowed to enter.

Even if an emergency repair was needed, repair men were not allowed on campus. One of our housekeeping staff became very proficient with most of our machines. Her husband, who was employed in the men's office of our college, would give her instructions at night on what he thought was wrong with the audio-visual equipment, air-conditioners or the photocopying machine. During the day, she would experiment from her memory of his instructions. On one occasion, we did have an air-conditioner fire resulting from amateur repairs.

Our college was planning to build a new class/office building for students and teachers. Among the plans considered was one in which the building would have had two lengthwise corridors with a row of classrooms in between. The classroom doors could be locked from either corridor, thus allowing boys to use the middle row of classrooms in the mornings and the girls could have classes there in the evenings, with the two sexes never seeing each other. It was decided that this sort of classroom building was too risky. Male and female non-Saudi faculty wanted to have our offices near each other in order to be able to consult on curriculum and all other things teachers need from each other. But this plan was discarded as being too hazardous. The implication was that all kinds of illegal and immoral consorting would occur.

At Riyadh International School, where most American youngsters went, during 1981, the staff was working to perfect something similar to our disaster drills, to deal with the potential visit of the mutawah. No school was supposed to conduct co-educational classes. Saudi law said no matter what the nationality, males and females absolutely must be separated for education. But, the fact that the American, French and British schools did have co-education was overlooked as long as no Muslim children were involved. Enrollment sheets were checked for religious affiliation. However, the Ministry of Education did inspect from time to time, usually giving a few days warning so classes could be safely sex-segregated before the inspectors arrived. The drill they were initiating was preparation in the event that no warning was given. At a certain signal, the boys would all go to one room with a male teacher and all the girls would go to an assigned female teacher and room. To avoid getting on the Ministry "bad-list" and consequently becoming the object of persecutory surprise inspections, they practiced the drill.

One American I met was the first woman to ever be hired by a Saudi advertising agency. It was forbidden for men and women to work side by side. They were making a little frosted glass cubicle for her in which she could lock herself away from the men, in order to comply with Saudi labor laws. But before it was completed, one day, someone raised the alarm that the "Mutawah is coming!" She, knowing the agency might be closed if she were found there not locked away from the men, scrambled under her desk to hide inside the unlocked cubicle. After some time, quiet reigned, so she crept out to find that there had not been a mutawah at all. This incident just illustrates how severely and carefully, or not, the code was adhered to.

The survival of the institution of Saudi polygamy amazes many Westerners. When I returned home, one of the most frequent questions I received was, "Did you meet any multiple wives?" Yes, I met them in all strata of society.

Sura IV Verse 3

Marry women of your choice,
Two, or three, or four;
But if ye fear that ye shall not
Be able to deal justly (with them),
Then only one, or (a captive)
That your right hand possess.
That will be more suitable,
To prevent you
From doing injustice..

Obviously, they believed this to be the revealed word of God. It would be hard to dissuade people away from something they think is godly. Reinforcement of that belief was a continuing process as is exemplified in the following by Professor Abdul Al-Omar (1975);

> It is a clear fact that Islam, by regulating polygamy, has treated women with justice and mercy. Islam preferred the interests of women taken altogether to the individual feeling of jealousy or grief which a wife suffers in cases of polygamy. Those who oppose polygamy are the real enemies of women, virtue and prophets of Allah who practiced polygamy according to the laws of Allah. p. 54

That was a pretty heavy injunction for any woman to go against. Most Saudi men I met, and that was few as I was not encouraged to meet men, by the time they were forty-five, had acquired a second wife. One of the patients with whom I worked was from a family with four wives. Two Saudi wives and their combined eight children lived in a one room flat. The two foreign wives shared another one room flat with their broods. Obviously the man was not rich. He was a guard at the King's palace. He earnestly tried to comply with the Prophet's injunction and example by treating the wives with equality among them. One of the most powerful and important doctors in the Kingdom had married an illiterate Bedouin girl when he was young. When he went out of the Kingdom to do a residency in his specialty, he brought back a female doctor from another Muslim country. A few months before I left, he took another wife, a young educated woman half his age. The difference between that situation and the similar ones in the West were that the Saudis just did not need to bother to divorce the old wife when they took a new wife as Westerners are required to do. The most glaring difference from many Western women's point of view is that women were not accorded the same privilege, multiple husbands.

The reader may wonder with the strict separation of the sexes, how men and women did manage to get together for the perpetuation of the race. As an example of this process, one of the students who was twenty six years old, way past Saudi marrying age which was more frequently fifteen or sixteen, met her future husband in the following way; a thirty six year old man from another city was looking for a wife and told some friends in Riyadh of his desire to be married. These friends were neighbors of the students and knew she was not married. They approached her father and asked if the family were interested. The family discussed it and responded in the affirmative. A meeting was arranged so the student might see this man. She liked what she saw, so a betrothal meeting was arranged. The faculty learned about it after that formality. The student seemed as glowing and eager as any Western girl announcing her engagement. I heard many men state that they would not find the country so intolerable if they were married. I came to the conclusion that marriage might make it more tolerable for a woman, too.

In another situation, one of the men in the University who, of course, worked in the men's office, mentioned to two of his colleagues that he wished he were married. These two knew of an unmarried teacher in the women's office. They told the man desirous of marriage about her, though of course, neither of them knew her personally. The young man was interested. So the two matchmakers took the opportunity one day when a professor from the women's was in the men's office on business, to tell her of the young man's desire and to request that she find out if the teacher were interested. The professor agreed to ask. The teacher was interested. At that same time twenty consultants from the USA and UK descended for a ten day workshop. During that time, the professor and the two matchmakers carried many messages back and forth between the two buildings, each enclosed in its separate set of walls one and one half blocks apart. The teacher asked the aspirant to write down some things about himself for her. He did. They agreed to meet. The teacher and her family invited him to visit them in their flat to meet each other. He was pleasantly surprised to see how lovely she was. They seemed pleased with each other. After the visit, the lists of requirements began to pass back and forth. On his list of requirements for her was "No tight sweaters," and "Only long skirts." There were other requirements of this ilk. She agreed to all of them which meant a considerable change in her style since she had been quite modish before this event. They gave a betrothal party in a hotel banquet room to which only married couples were invited. Even this mixed party was an innovation.

I had no opportunity to attend a betrothal party but one student reported hers in the following way: All of her family was present. The father of the prospective groom was required to ask the bride how much money she wanted to be married to his son. Well, the student had known the young man for several years and felt herself to be in love with him. So she told her own father "I don't want anything in order to marry him." He father said to her in sotto voice, "What, you don't want anything!" Then her sisters said they would all be shamed if she were to be married without any gold. After a little coercion, the student asked her prospective father-in-law for forty thousand riyals or about twelve thousand American dollars. On her wedding day, she went to the hotel wedding room wearing no jewelry. The wedding guests then presented her with so much gold that by the time she left the party she was weighted down with it.

After I attended one Saudi wedding, I made the following entry in my journal the next day:

> We arrived about 8 pm and were greeted by the bride and grooms' mothers. Later three of the bride's sisters came to greet my friend who had taken me along as her guest. I wish I had words vivid enough to describe it. The room was full of women. Everyone had a fancy dress, the kind we wear to Christmas parties, with mountains of sequins, glitter, and gold embroidery and covered with gold jewelry. Several were wearing the kind of gold necklace that is like a chain mail bib of gold from neck to waist. Others wore a kind of glove of gold that actually is a series of rings on each finger and a wrist band connected to each ring by chains which have a jewel encrusted discs on each link. And then each woman also had a black face veil or face cloth on or near her head. The moment a man came in to bring more chairs, up went the face clothes, sometimes just sideways to shield just the side of the face toward the man. The children, and there were batches of them, were all dressed up, too; the girls in miniature wedding dresses seemingly which made me think they were practicing. Some black serving women came carrying huge trays of cups for Arabic coffee which in this case was really just cardamom and saffron, no coffee at all. It was quite tasty. I had two cups.
>
> There was an all woman band with the leader playing an instrument like a large mandolin which I learned later is called an *ude*. The rest of the band played percussion and/or sang. My friend said that they were "love songs!" The band had arrived about 9 pm. Every time a serving man came into the room, the musicians got those face clothes up without missing a beat. I never did figure out how they did that. It really looked strange to see seven musicians playing like mad with a black cloth wrapped completely around and over each face, while they sat on the stage and sang into microphones.
>
> About 10:45 pm, the wedding procession came in led by about twelve little girls in the miniature white wedding dresses, carrying huge tapers that were lit. I was so worried lest one of them light her hair or dress on fire. Once they got into place on either side of the bridal couple, and the photographer finished, they put the tapers out and I breathed a sigh of relief. The bride and groom sat up on a stage in two big carved upholstered

chairs banked with <u>artificial</u> flowers. A couple of relatives came up and gave gold to the bride. Then the groom opened a brief case type thing and took out one of those gold bibs and put it around the bride's neck. That was it! The ceremony was over. They got up and went out into another banquet room where about twenty square yards of table were solidly covered with food. The wedding guests followed the couple into the feast. Within twenty minutes, the table was a shambles of half filled plates, overturned Pepsi cans and empty serving vessels. The bridal couple had by then disappeared.

Unless one were a Muslim, it was not possible to marry within the Kingdom. Many Westerners flew to Cyprus to legalize their relationships. On occasion, the Christian minister would perform a ceremony, but it was not a legal ceremony under Saudi law. They would have another ceremony outside the Kingdom. The American consul reported that many Americans requested to be married in the embassy in Jeddah and were dismayed to find that it was not legal. We think of our embassy as a bit of American soil, but not according to Saudi law.

The possibility of sex outside of marriage was not a subject for discussion. The society acted as if sex within marriage was the only way it ever happened. In the Nursing Department where I taught, it was forbidden to discuss either birth control or evolution. During a technological era, where their five year plans included mind-boggling schemes for building, it seemed incongruous that the main focus of their social energies were spent on separation of the sexes, rather than on improvement of the quality of life for all.

REFERENCES:

Ali, Abdallah Yousef (1931) *The Quran*, Egypt.

Al-Omar, Abdul (1975). *Islam: The Religion of Truth*. Kingdom of Saudi Arabia: The Supreme Head Office for Religious Researches, Ifta, Call, and Guidance Departments.

Beck, Lois & Keddie, Nikki (1978) *Women in the Muslim World*. Cambridge, MA: Harvard University Press.

Salahi, Adil (January 1, 1982). "Women and Islam". *Arab News*

Watt, W. Montgomery (1961). *Islam and the Integration of Society*. London: Routledge & Kegan Paul, Ltd.

7

HEALTH AND HEALTH CARE

Some of the diseases I saw which we Americans seldom see anymore were polio, malaria, trachoma, schistosomiasis, bilharzia, thalassemia, typhoid and tuberculosis. Because my time was spent in hospitals or hospital related teaching, I was very wary of having health matters dominate this book. Indeed, another book could be written about research, new equipment and its misuse and traditional Arab medicine. This included branding a painful limb or organ with a hot iron. However, a more important aspect to me was how religion and culture which permeated all of life there, affected the health care.

Sura V Verse 7
Ye who believe!
When ye prepare
For prayer, wash
Your faces, and your hands
(And arms) to the elbow;
Rub your heads (with water);
And (wash) your feet
To the ankles.
If ye are in a state
Of ceremonial impurity*
Bath your whole body.
But if ye are ill, or on a journey,

59

Or one of you cometh
From the offices of nature,
Or ye have been in contact with women,
And ye find no water,
Then take for yourselves
Clean sand or earth,
And rub therewith
Your faces and hands.
God doth not wish
To place you in a difficulty,
To make you clean,
And to complete
His favor to you,
That ye may be grateful.

*The translator of my Koran (Ali, 1931) defines ceremonial impurity as arising from "sex pollution".

It becomes pretty obvious that women and contact with them was equated with "the offices of nature". Abdullah Ali (1931) was very clear in his footnote, what constituted ceremonial impurity; sex. And sex meant women since the *sura* does not direct women to bath after contact with men. Women were equated with illness, a journey or defecation. The overall behavior of the women in Saudi Arabia, the acquiescence with these extremes of degradation showed that they had assimilated the idea, after centuries of being told they were equal to excretory products. The popular saying attributed to the Catholic priest in the USA is "Give me a child until he is five, and he will be mine for life," expresses the same idea I wish to convey. These women have centuries rather than years of receiving the message that they are feces (shit). The human growth and development theorists of the 20th century such as Piaget, Maslow, Giselle and Freud all echo the same thought: "You will be what you are told you are during your early years."

Sura XVI Verse 68
And thy Lord taught the Bee
To build its cells in hills,
On trees, and in (men's) habitations;

Verse 69
Then to eat of all

The produce (of the earth),
And find with skill the spacious
Paths of its Lord: there issues
From within their bodies
A drink of varying colors (This refers to honey)
Wherein is healing for men:
Verily in this is a Sign
For those who give thought.

The hexagonal shape of the honeycomb is frequent in Islamic art, almost as if they were trying to compete with the bee for the favor of God. Islamic art had so many ways of stretching and varying the same shape or theme that the designs achieve almost the height of the mandala, which is "a ritual geometric diagram, sometimes corresponding to a specific attribute . . . which is thus given visual expression" (Cirlot 1962). This may be an idea that the Muslims borrowed from the older Hindu culture. With trade routes being what they were, they undoubtedly were influenced by that ancient religion. But, to return to honey as a healer, it was a common ingredient in many cakes and pastries, though I never heard it discussed as having particularly healing qualities until I was back in the USA and met a physiology professor from Libya. Arabs have gotten so far away from the simple diet of dates, laban and bread that was common forty years ago, that they may have lost this idea of honey having healing properties.

Sura XVII Verse 82

We send down (stage by stage)
In the Qur'an that which
Is a healing and a mercy
To those who believe:
To the unjust it causes
Nothing but loss after loss.

Sura XLI Verse 19

On the Day that
The enemies of God
Will be gathered together
To the Fire, they will
Be marched in ranks.

Verse 20
At length, when they reach
The (Fire), their hearing,
Their sight, and their skins
Will bear witness against them,
As to (all) their deeds.

In working closely with Saudi patients with permanent disabilities, I learned from them that they believed their afflictions were a direct result of not following Allah's wishes. One patient reported to me that on several occasions, friends and family had commented to him that he must have been very evil for Allah to have punished him so. The patient said that he, too, came to believe his accident had been a punishment. However, this seemed not to have changed his approach to life as I never saw him praying or reading the Koran as I often saw other patients do.

This attitude of illness as punishment made it pretty hard to implement rehabilitation programs, let alone primary or preventive health care. If it is punishment to be sick or injured, then it is God's Will and there is no way to duck it. *En Sha Allah* or "according to God's Will" was the comment I heard most frequently during my residence. This attitude permeated the way patients approached rehabilitation. When I would begin to discuss ways of making themselves more independent, they would respond with the idea that if God wanted them to be more independent, he would cause them to improve. It's pretty hard to buck God in somebody's mind; unequal competition. McNeill (1979) writes:

> By the sixteenth century, when Christian rules of quarantine and other prophylactic measures against plague had attained firm definition, Moslem views hardened against efforts to escape the will of Allah.

My first experience with attitudes about health care in Saudi Arabia came during my interview in Houston. On of the few questions I asked my interviewer was "What is the life expectancy in Saudi Arabia?" I had already read several books and in none of them could I find a figure regarding life expectancy. His response was "What is life expectancy?" This, from a man who had his PhD in laboratory science, shocked me. But I thought it was a language problem, despite the fact that otherwise, his English was good. After I had been in the country for some months, I heard casually that the life expectancy for men was forty- seven years but that for women, it was much younger due to their heavy childbearing under less than ideal conditions, but nobody even suggested an exact figure for women. However, in all fairness, I must say that with the rapid advances and willingness to spend money for tertiary health care, life expectancy rate were expected to rise rapidly. It was only after many months in Saudi Arabia that I learned that not only had they not kept such records until recently, but when the did synthesize such figures, they were a carefully guarded secret, not to be shared with the world at large, not even with the World Health Organization.

From my journal of December 1980, I took the following story:

> "Yesterday, at work, we found out that our little cleaning girl, a Black Bedouin from Najran, had died on Thursday in the main hospital for commoners here. She acted sick at work on Tuesday. Her eye looked swollen and she sat most of the day trying to catch a spot of sun, looking oh, so sick. One of the nursing faculty made the secretary call the cleaning supervisor and instruct them to send a car to take her to the hospital. She was probably only seventeen years old. She looked twenty at the outside. Women seem to look older than their age here rather than the opposite. I suppose it is the bad diet, bad health practices and wouldn't we all look older if we were banned from doing everything except have babies? But this little young thing died of "heart failure"! Probably she had a rheumatic heart. Apparently many of them do! And the Bedouin girls start working so young, like ten years of age."

Then I went on to describe her replacement;

> "So yesterday also, we got a new set of sisters to clean, etc. I came out of my office when I heard a ruckus in the hall and found these two Black Bedouins examining my plastic and paper mache' anatomical models. And tasting the blue chalk! Another faculty member was trying to tell them it is OK to have these bodies exposed like that. Islam bans exposure of the body and dissection of cadavers. Finally she just said to them "Cover your faces" so that they would not have to see the bodies. Well, she just walked away and the girls were still looking avidly, so I just began to disassemble the model for them and show them by sign language, the heart and lungs. I then said to them in Arabic "paper and plastic", some of my few Arabic words and they appeared to be satisfied. I can't really understand Arabic yet, but it is obvious to me in that short encounter, that their

accent is different and difficult to even hear, let alone pick out a few words. But they appeared to understand my few words, except I saw the blue chalk on the floor in their room as if they were saving it to taste again tomorrow. I told them 'NO' to chalk eating."

I later learned first hand that the statement about Islam banning exposure and dissection of cadavers is not true. On one occasion I was required to visit the office of the head of the anatomy department as the men's campus and as I walked by the laboratory, I looked in the open door and saw a blackish cadaver on the dissecting table. This occurred six months after the above episode. I could find no references in the Koran in regard to this treatment of dead bodies.

Their regulations regarding separation of the sexes caused many problems for them in their health care system. One Saudi female professional employed in an administrative position quite high in the education ministry, was barred from attending a conference in a hotel where new machines and technology for amplifying sound were being shown and demonstrated. In her position as supervisor of deaf education for girls, she expected to be allowed to view these new aides for hearing. Upon attempting to find out what days women were allowed to attend, she found that they were not allowed to attend at all. Thus, they deprived her of gaining expertise and effectively kept her from being as aware as her male colleagues of the current developments within the field. Situations such as this occurred throughout the health care professions. Inevitably, this would further widen the already existing gap between health care for males and health care for females, as Saudis prefer that most health care for women be done by female professionals, who are deprived of current information.

An instance of the inequality of care for the sexes occurred in the special treatment unit for the spinal cord injured where I worked. The main treatment unit housed only male patients. Female spinal cord injured patients were segregated as is customary and were placed in a female orthopedic unit at the other end of the hospital. Specialized staff members were assigned to the male unit. It meant a five minute walk to the other end of the hospital to see the women patients. The specially trained therapists and nursing staff just did not have time from their busy schedules with their own patients to attend to these women. Therefore, their therapy and care was done by the regular unit staff. The result was that their independence and rehabilitation was sadly inferior to the males. Examples of this sort occurred throughout the Ministry of Health facilities. However, the hospitals administered by American and British management firms used Western standards of care which generally meant treatment was not segregated except in specific instances; female surgical wards and male surgical wards were near each other with identical facilities.

Duplication of health services occurred because of sex-segregation in the same way it did in the education system. According to Graham Benton (1982):

> There are a dozen different government agencies and philanthropic organizations running their own health services. The Defense Ministry and the National Guard, for instance provide cradle-to-the-grave care for their employees and families, while King Faisal Hospital is funded by the King Faisal Foundation. Not surprisingly, this tends to lead to duplication of services and sometimes neglect of vitally necessary health care. The government has established a National Health Council to supervise and coordinate the activities of the health agencies.

That was the first I knew of this National Health Council and I was working in a facility run by the Ministry of Health as well as one run by the Ministry of Higher Education. Both could be expected to have disseminated this information to faculty and staff training health professionals. Neither did. It was a common occurrence for events of this momentous importance to our various health professions to occur without the people most affected being informed.

There was no organized channel for informing people of decisions affecting them, either in health care, education or police enforcement. I knew of it when the edict was enforced upon me. This method or lack of method may hark back to the nomadic days when the only news a person heard was around the campfire when other travelers happened by, by chance. Most information in health care was passed "by chance" or so it seemed to me. Our oft repeated adage "Ignorance is no excuse" would definitely not be fair in Saudi Arabia because of the lack of organized information systems.

Benton (1982) went on to discuss our programs:

> On paper, too, educational programs are impressive. Its main difficulty is finding the qualified teachers and requisite pupils at all levels when commercial opportunities look more attractive than academic or vocational study.

This problem was apparent in both the hospital and the University. The World Health Organization had several training programs for paraprofessionals in the hospital and though they would enroll Saudi students, their class attendance was erratic; their clinical work sporadic and casual. It was difficult to find staff in the hospital adequately trained and motivated to supervise them. They were not easy to supervise. So though they were enrolled in training, the quality was questionable and it was doubtful that most graduates would be competent to operate the basic procedures without continued assistance from ex-patriot professionals or paraprofessionals. That was a disappointing end to several years of training. Part of the problem was that Saudi students could and did voice their dissatisfaction with teachers or programs by going straight to the King, the Director or the Dean. Therefore, most foreigners felt vulnerable to this complaint process and were reluctant to enforce student regulations. The students got the idea that they were indeed more powerful than their teachers and need not abide by rules given by foreigners. These situations caused feelings of helplessness in the faculty and hence produced low staff morale and high turn-over.

Nursing and hospital care for the sick had its start in the Middle East. The Christian Crusaders came, saw, and liked the idea so took it back to Europe where they started the first Western hospitals with Catholic 'Sisters'. Then in the last few centuries when Europeans successfully colonized the Middle East, they carried the idea of nursing back to its origin. Between the Crusades and the exportation of the Florence Nightingale image in the nineteenth century, nursing in the Middle East sank in status and was equated with prostitution. It has just begun to regain its place professionally. In Saudi Arabia where slavery was legal until 1962, nurses most frequently were slaves. So it may take a while for a nurse to be accepted as other than a prostitute or slave in Saudi Arabia. One educated Saudi mother told me, "I would never allow my son to marry a nurse." Our Saudi students on many different occasions told me that, "No man will marry me because of my profession." But I learned that that was not true since three married and five became betrothed during my association with them. When we moved our Nursing Department of the University from a villa of classrooms onto the main "female" campus, our students reported that the other female students, liberal arts, psychology, sociology, social work and education expressed some very negative feelings about having nursing students in such close proximity. We set out on a public relations campaign to win them over. We invited them in, gave them tours of the Nursing Building, after we had first scrubbed the building from top to bottom since it was filthy when we moved in. We three American faculty members tried to teach our Egyptian and Sudanese cleaning crew how to clean. They said "Yes," took the cleaning equipment we had purchased from our own pockets and then they never used them. We did not try to requisition the cleaning supplies we favored as it would have taken years to get them. So we bought new cleaning supplies and equipment and started over to find the cleaners were furious with us for demeaning ourselves and for doing their jobs. But eventually, we got the building 'ship-shape' and were complimented by staff from other departments on the exemplary condition of our building. Our cleaning staff never saw us the same way again because they gradually ceased providing some of the little services they had previously done, while they continued to provide them to the Middle Eastern faculty who had not participated in the cleaning. Doing servant's work had changed our image. But we felt vindicated when gradually, the rest of the campus began to look better, cleaner and we recognized some of our cleaning techniques in operation.

One of the fallout situations from the historical image of the nurse as whore and slave was that in the Ministry of Health and Ministry of Higher Education facilities, nurses and physical therapists were essentially locked up. It was not that they were actually locked up, rather that they lived in dormitories called hostels from which they were only allowed to leave for short scheduled times. Different hostels had different rules, and the rules changed quickly and drastically if there was the slightest infraction. The Filipina 'Sisters' with whom I worked were allowed three hours of shopping on Thursday evenings which are like Saturday nights in America, the evening before the Sabbath. They could not go out between 7 am and 7 pm on Friday, the Sabbath. If they were more than fifteen minutes late, the whole hostel would be punished by being deprived of their free time the following weekend. The South Korean 'Sisters' lived under an even more repressive system. They were allowed to go out to the souq in a hospital mini-bus for two hours every two weeks, other wise they were confined to their block of flats. On one occasion, I met one of the physical therapists in a downtown bookstore during those two hours in order to have a chance to visit together away from work. I asked the Korean therapist if I might not be allowed to come home with them some afternoon after work and possibly eat lunch with them. The answer was "No," their Matron would not even allow me, one of their co-workers, to visit them inside their hostel. That seemed very like a jail to me. During my last weeks there, one of the Korean 'Sisters' met her Korean boyfriend during the bi-weekly two hour shopping time and went for a ride in his car. They had an accident. He was killed and she was severely injured. The entire hostel was confined for the next month. No shopping!

At the University Hospital under the Ministry of Higher Education, the Filipina nurses, dental assistants and other allied health professionals were housed in flats approximately two blocks away from the hospital. They were given the injunction that they must always walk in groups of four, not less, to insure that they would not do 'bad things' on their way home. And indeed I would see them walking in their quartets but occasionally one member of the group was male. No matter how they tried to keep men and women apart, 'Nature' would intervene.

American and British nurses would not tolerate being locked up, though they tried unsuccessfully. I found it upsetting that those that I worked with and became close to were locked up. I began to cogitate upon the inhumanity of locking up working professionals. I wondered why the World Health Organization had never done anything to alleviate this situation. I began to ask why there was no nurse consultant in Saudi Arabia when they had a physical therapist consultant and an orthopedic/prosthetic consultant. Surely nurses were more primary in healthcare than either of the above, yet they had not had one. Why? The answer: The Ministry of Health had never asked for one, apparently not seeing the need. So I decided the best thing I could do for Saudi Arabia and for my conscience was to try to get the Ministry to ask for a nurse consultant, and eventually, when the conditions for nurses became known formally to the World Health Organization, they might be able to shame the Saudis into better treatment of their professionals. When I asked the doctors if it would not be possible to request a WHO nurse consultant, their response was "For what?" I had to think quickly to come up with some plausible reasons, since my primary reason would not seem reasonable to Saudi doctors, who keep their own women so well locked up. Certainly, there were many areas of need for nursing in-service education, so it was not difficult to make a list of needs. The doctors needed constant reminding in order to be motivated to ask the Ministry. The administration of the hospital changed and I was unable to accomplish this goal before my departure.

One day while I was supervising students in the hospital, I saw them in a very animated conversation which they repeated to me in English. There were three of them. A famous imam, religious teacher, Sheik Abd al-Aziz bin Baz, who was blind, had been brought into the girls' hostel at the University to talk to the students. "If he wasn't blind, he would never have been allowed into that jail," I wrote in my journal. He had talked to the students about dress. Firstly he had said that at the pre-betrothal meeting, the only one at which the man is able to see the woman since she is always supposed to be covered up, that the woman should show her neck, arms and legs to the knees such as is possible when a Western style dress is worn, so that he has the opportunity to see her before signing the betrothal contract. They then went on to tell me that he had also spoken especially to the nursing and medical students saying they should cover their faces all except one eye while treating patients in the hospital. Now wouldn't that be a kick, giving injections with only one eye. No binocular vision, no depth perception! The mental image seemed hilarious. Our students at that time covered only their hair in addition to wearing their uniforms. They had a choice of hair covers. Some wore a black silk scarf around their head and neck; some wore a specially shaped thing that made them look like a nun except their uniforms were white pantsuits. Or they could wear a kind of modified bonnet type nurse's cap which fit down over their whole head. The students were indignant about what the imam had said. They discussed the contradictions between the two sets of instruction. They were irate that he should suggest that they could give patient care with one eye while holding all that bunch of cloth from the long veil in one hand. They went on to say he had said that women should treat only women and men treat only men. The students then vociferously expostulated about how men doctors would still continue to see women patients. It just meant that women doctors and nurses would not be able to treat men patients. Their awareness of the situation is a hopeful sign. However, during the few months following the appearance of the blind imam in the hostel, I began to see a few medical students attending clinical classes on our unit with a face mask similar to the Bedouin mask, with the cotton veil hanging from a forehead band with cords to cover the lower half of the face while leaving the eyes uncovered. Before he made this edict, I had never seen students or staff covering their faces while working in hospitals or clinics. Now they were doing so. The imam apparently affected some students with his lecture. 'One step forward and two steps back' was how I felt about this outcome.

On another occasion, when we took our students for a visit to the clinic run by the American Army Corp of Engineers, we saw a new waiting room for females, just like the Saudi clinics. It had not been there on our previous visit. Upon inquiring, we were told that the clinic had just been refused licensure by the Saudi government because it did not comply with all the regulations, specifically, it did not have separate-sex waiting rooms. There were three classes of medical facilities eligible for licensure, hospitals, clinics and dispensaries. They qualified for almost all the items on the dispensary list except waiting rooms, enough servants and cleaning personnel. In their attempt to become legal, they had designated one of the former patient rooms as a female waiting room.

While they can buy all the expensive equipment that makes them look as if they are moving forward in the medical world, in fact, many of their religious conflicts prevent them from real progress.

REFERENCES:

Ali, Abdallah Yousef (1931) *The Quran,* Egypt.

Benton, Graham (April 1982). Health Care; Special Treatment. *The Middle East Magazine,* No. 90.

Cirlot, J. E. (1962). *A Dictionary of Symbols.* London: Kegan Paul Ltd.

McNeill, William H. (1979). *Plagues and People.* Middlesex, Great Britain: Penguin Books.

8

MONEY, WORK and STATUS

⁂

Sura XVII Verse 30
Verily thy Lord doth provide
Sustenance in abundance
For whom He pleaseth, and He
Provideth in a just measure.
For He doth know
And regard his servants.

The Koranic injunctions about work are few enough that I concluded that work, as we know it in the West, did not comprise an important part of their idea about how to live life. The work referred to in the Koran, was the work of furthering Islam. By all appearances, they had no "work ethic". From a Western point of view, this was a <u>lack</u>. We have our Horatio Alger stories, our ideas of alleviating sadness by hard work, our vocational rehabilitation centers, vocational training centers and a history of "hard labor" as rehabilitative punishment. By contrast, punishment for them meant lashing or beheading. While I perceive the difference, I confess difficulty in avoiding giving their concept of punishment a negative judgment.

When we Westerners think of our mental image when someone says hard work, the usual picture that comes to mind is of someone using tools such as ditch-digging or lawn mowing. We have been using tools for centuries. The Arabs, and especially the Saudis have used few tools except weapons, camel sticks, waterwheels, looms or mud-masonry tools up until the oil drillers arrived. Consequently, our dexterity with tools and our expectations for the products of their use have had centuries to develop while theirs have had a few decades. We speak in our Western cultures about how to modify the "work ethic" to be compatible with automation, while in Saudi Arabia they spoke of how to stimulate the "work ethic". The breadth of contrast between Saudi and Western attitudes about work came second only to their ideas about males and females.

Historically, raiding was more important than working. W. Montgomery Watt concludes:

> Even from a comparatively early period, the proceeds of raids were an important part of the finances of the Islamic state, for a fifth of the value of any spoils taken had to be paid to Muhammad as administering the public treasury of the community.

My own personal experience and opinion were that the raiding attitude continued in the sphere of commerce and labor practices in 1982. If a Saudi could trick you out of money, he would because culturally it was OK despite the following;

Sura LXXXIII Verse 1
Woe to those
That deal in fraud.

Stealing was not OK, but tricking us was. Unfortunately for them, they have learned the hard way that professionals from Western countries were highly assertive and resentful about being tricked. A letter by four laboratory technologists to their professional journal successfully blocked recruitment efforts in Britain in 1982. Those from poorer Middle Eastern countries like Egypt and Pakistan, no matter how they were tricked, found pay and conditions better in Saudi Arabia than at home and so they tolerated such trickery. The Saudi's success with those less fortunate, less assertive but more numerous people, gave them the idea that all expatriates could be treated in that cavalier fashion. Only after they found increasing difficulty with hiring did they learn that these labor policies did not work with people accustomed to regular government inspection and regulation of labor practices.

The work week was from Saturday to Wednesday. Perhaps half the population worked one half of Thursday, which is like our Saturday since

Friday is their Sabbath. My contract specified that I would work thirty-five hours per week in instruction, research, academic counseling and other academic duties. However, most people outside the University that I knew, worked from 7:30 am to 1:30 pm, and then went home to rest during the extremely hot part of the day, then came back to work at 5:00 pm until 8:00 pm., so that the work day was nine hours long. That kind of schedule made attending evening functions difficult if not impossible. But that schedule would fit for a culture where entertainments were usually outlawed. In the 1940s, mutawahs, the religious police, still had the right and frequently did enter homes if they heard music or smelled cigarette smoke. They beat the offender with their staff. I heard reports that in the more provincial towns and villages, this practice was still observed in 1982. While <u>work</u> might not be the ethic, neither was <u>pleasure.</u>

In *The World Press Review,* (July 1981) there was an article called "Saudi Arabia's Race with Time". The staff writer referred to "A class of pampered Saudis and a sub-class of insecure foreign helots." That was how many Westerners felt about themselves and other expatriates, when they called themselves "the Golden Slaves". All possible administrative positions were filled with Saudis regardless of the absence of training or background. Despite the fact that they consequently made many mistakes and poor judgments, the expatriates usually got the blame. A frequent warning heard was "The Saudis will never cause each other to lose face". Expatriates got the blame for the very problems they had anticipated and warned the Saudis about. For example, one American construction engineer and manager had his best craftsmen taken by his Saudi bosses to work on other of their own projects, thus causing his project to be unfinished in time. They berated him while refusing to acknowledge that they were causing the delay. Jean Baker Miller M.D. (1976) made the following point regarding dominance:

> Dominant groups usually define one or more acceptable roles for the subordinates. Acceptable roles typically involve providing services that no dominant group wants to perform for itself (for example, cleaning up the dominants' waste products). Functions that a dominant group prefers to perform, on the other hand, are carefully guarded and closed to subordinates. Out of the total range of human possibilities, the activities most highly valued in any particular culture will tend to be enclosed within the domain of the dominant group; less valued functions are relegated to the subordinates. p.6

That pretty accurately describes what went on in the Saudi Arabian work force. The Saudis held all the top positions. Their College of Administrative Sciences at the University of Riyadh, now King Saud University, was one of the biggest, with three thousand students according to the 1979 Twentieth Anniversary catalogue from the College of Administrative Sciences. It was one of the first colleges in the University. Administration was much more of a priority than medicine, which was not started until ten years later.

The service functions, like nursing, street cleaning, garbage collection, agricultural labor and maintenance were for the most part, performed by foreign laborers, with Yemenis at the bottom of the 'work, status, money' hierarchy and advancing upward to Pakistanis, Egyptians, Eritreans, Ethiopians, Koreans, Filipinos, Sudanese, and then Egyptian professionals, Palestinians, Jordanians, with Westerners at the top of the pile just under the Saudis. This subjective view was commonly held by most of my multi-national acquaintances.

Another example of the "top dog" policy of the Saudis was in commerce. Every business had to have a Saudi counterpart, partner or sponsor. This meant practically, that foreign business men came and organized things, did the work, sustained the stress and gave half, if not more of the profits to the Saudi sponsor. In many cases, the Saudi left the entire management end to the Westerner and appeared in his office once or twice per month., just often enough to overrule business decisions made by the Western manager. On one such occasion, a manager of several grocery stores had his decision for maintaining a level of stock in the warehouse overruled so they waited to reorder an item after it was finished and it would take several months for it to arrive. This policy became visibly obvious by the missing items on the store shelves. The store personnel would say "Next week, God Willing!" when I asked about an item absent from the shelves. We westerners expected shelves to be constantly stocked as most are in the US stores.

The *Saudi Labor and Workmen Law* (1980) approved by the Council of Ministers in 1970 and still used in 1982 provided for regulation of labor conditions. It included everyone except those working in family enterprises, agricultural workers and domestics. Like Americans, they could legally treat farm workers with disregard for recognized labor practices applicable to other industries. However, we do not have a servant/domestic class for the most part, or we did not in 1982. That era had passed for us, anyway most of us who did our own childcare, laundry and cooking. But the Saudis could keep servants locked within their villas and did so. During one wedding party I attended, a pale Filipina approached me and asked if I spoke English. She seated herself beside me. She informed me that she was the 'nurse' for the spoiled little boy who kept disrupting the dancing. She went on to say that she was forbidden to use the telephone, to leave the walls surrounding the villa unless a family member was with her and was there anything I could do to help her? Well, there was nothing I could do, except to ask if there was any way she could contact the Filipino Embassy. Little did I know that the Filipino Embassy did nothing for workers like that as it was apparently in a poor negotiating position with the Saudis. Only the Filipinos working for the Ministry of Health and Higher Education are under contract with Embassy sanction and are therefore entitled to protection, according to Filipino health workers I knew. Over the years, the Saudis had the tradition of slavery and servitude, abolishing legal slavery in 1962. Many who came to Saudi Arabia to make the pilgrimage sold children to pay for their return trip to their homelands. It was a multi-national group. Because the Koran sanctioned slavery, the Saudi Arabs apparently felt that this form of human exploitation was proper. Old habits die hard. This attitude toward slavery/servitude caused difficulty when people from countries who long ago abolished slavery worked in Saudi Arabia. One such case was that of Prince Turki Bin Abdul Aziz (*Newsweek*, 1982) a former Deputy Defense Minister, was charged by Dade County, Florida law enforcement officials with requiring" his servants to surrender their passports." Keeping the passport of a foreign national is a breach of the Geneva Conventions. However, all Saudi government employees surrendered their passports to their employers also. The University held my passport requiring a two month Salary as bond before they would give it to me, or a contract signed by another University employee that they would pay the two month bond if I failed to return and fulfill my contract. The *Newsweek* article went on to say that Prince Turki "had been the subject of newspaper stories alleging that he virtually imprisoned his household servants, forcing them to work seven days a week at low wages." That sort of treatment of domestics was tolerated and was in fact legal in Saudi Arabia though it may have not been sanctioned elsewhere. The ironic part was that we who entered their Kingdom to work signed documents that we would abide by the Shariah, Islamic law while we were there and were severely punished if found violating it, while Prince Turki was granted diplomatic immunity from prosecution for violating US laws.

There were poor people in the Kingdom, despite reports to the contrary. Many Americans have the idea that everyone in Saudi Arabia is rich. I saw evidence of what we consider "poverty" everywhere; shacks on vacant lots, people scavengering the garbage dumpsters and garbage cans and people, sleeping in the open. However, American standards of 'poverty' cannot be applied to Bedouin recently off the desert.

In my journal in April, 1981, I wrote the following;

The greatest bunches of foreign nurses here are Egyptian, Korean, and Filipinas. And English is the second language in all those countries. So they are able to function in a system that keeps records in English. Ministry of Health records in Saudi Arabia are kept in both English and Arabic. I learned this later when I actually started to work in the hospital. The Egyptians come because their own salaries and standard of living is so low. Salaries here are fantastic compared to their own. For Americans, these salaries aren't fantastic, just pretty good. Now the Koreans come for a different reason. The best export Korea has is labor, their national resource. So they have a trade agreement with Saudi Arabia, that Korea will supply a certain number of healthy laborers for so many months each year. So then Korea turns around and drafts their laborers and nurses, something like our Peace Corp, but there is no choice about it. The Koreans here are required to send home to their families two thirds of what they make here. *This non-choice statement I later learned was erroneous. They had either the option of taking their national service either with the Korean military or on one of these international labor contracts. And they were paid 10% here while 90% went home.* And of course, the government receives some benefits from the Saudi government, too, probably oil and money.

The national characteristics of the various workers probably followed the same work patterns they had in their homelands. The Filipinos were vigorous and thorough workers by most standards. Most of them were supporting a family at home in the Philippines. The Koreans, perhaps because they were "impressed" into service, tended to be a little more lackadaisical and superficially obedient to authority. The Egyptians tended to function a little more slowly, as is customary for people from extremely hot, disease ridden countries. The British maintained a stiff upper lip through it all. Americans went around performing in our usual aggressive, high-blood pressure producing way. Except for me! I enjoyed the 7:30-2:30 routine. I became addicted to afternoon naps. Would I ever be able to work ala American again? I wondered.

Because of the great changes that have taken place in the last twenty years since the inception of female education, it is important to further discuss females in the work place. Beck and Keddie (1978) state that;

Discrimination on the job and at home is least at the top levels. Female doctors, lawyers, artists, professors, teachers, nurses, secretaries, other professionals and even high level government personnel are to be found in the Muslim countries significantly influenced by modernization, though their absolute numbers may be small. p. 10

While Saudi Arabia is in the Muslim World, the above statement fell a little short of describing the situation there. Women were not allowed to be in the 'top' in any field of work. For example the highest woman at the university could only be a vice dean as women were not allowed to be deans. Women heading departments for females in government ministries were called 'supervisors', not department heads, though the work may have been the same. The results of that situation were that, though the Saudis allege that there is equal pay for women, when the job name changed, the pay scale changed. Doctors as the same level received the same pay in hospitals; it was just that females did not become heads of departments; therefore they were not eligible for the big money.

Women were also deprived another way. I hear men claim that forty to fifty percent of Saudi wealth was controlled by women. This seemed unreasonable to me since women died earlier and inherit half the portion given to men and were unable to function in those positions where commissions were paid.

Sura IV Verse 7
From what is left by parents
And those nearest related
There is a share for women,
Whether the property be small
Or large, --a determinate share.

Verse 11
(Inheritance); to the male,
A portion equal to that,
Of two females: if only
Daughters, two or more,
Their share is two thirds
Of the inheritance:
If only one, her share
Is a half.

One Saudi married couple that I knew, who had studied for their masters degrees in a leading American university, had been hired into the respective men's and women's section of a government agency. In that rare situation, the Saudi woman was supervised by an American woman. We American women had fewer restrictions on us regarding meeting Saudi men face to face. One day, upon returning from a departmental meeting with the male director, the American woman informed the Saudi woman that the director would like to meet with her. I was astonished to learn that the Saudi woman had been hired sight unseen, until I remembered that Saudi women are to be seen by no men but their husbands and *maharram*. I thought that surely, several years in an American university, sitting in coeducational classes would have loosened this barrier, but the American woman's request was followed by this conversation:

> **Saudi Woman**: I don't know. I'll have to ask my husband.

> **American Woman Supervisor:** But you can cover your face and I'll be there.

> **Saudi Woman:** I'll have to ask my husband.

> **American Woman Supervisor**: Well, your husband can be there, too, with me and the director and your face covered.

> **Saudi Woman**: I'll have to ask my husband.

> **American Woman Supervisor**: OK, ask your husband.

> **Me**: It sounds like the director just wanted Jane to sound you out on whether you could meet him.

> **Saudi Woman**: (nodding) Oh, yes, of course, he wanted to have Jane ask me so I could mention it to my husband, so when the director asks him if he can meet me, my husband won't be shocked and insulted.

Men never mentioned their wives directly to other unrelated men. It is permissible to ask about another man's family, but never directly asking or mentioning the wife. In this changing society, where women were beginning to be employed by men, this sort of problem arose. The director in the previously described situation was doing his best to cover himself both culturally and administratively. Very complex, when both old and new standards must be met!

Once educated, female Saudi university graduates may never work. The husband of one of our students who married before graduation, agreed to allow her to finish her schooling including her year of internship, but he said she would never be able to work in a hospital, perhaps teaching in the University, but never the hospital. This may be the eventual outcome for many females graduating in the 1980s just like American university graduates in the 1930s and 1940s. Nadi Youssef (1978) made the following statement regarding male attitudes toward Muslim women working;

> Educated Muslim men admitted that their objection to female employment rested in their lack of confidence in married women. The persistent mistrust was explained as resulting from the arranged marriage system, where family pressure often prevails over the will of either spouse. In the men's own words there is no reason for having confidence in a woman whom you know has married you in obedience to her parent's wishes, or because there was nothing else for her to do. p. 92.

Youseff may have been stating the unconscious view expressed by many Muslim men regarding their fear of wives working. However, it seems a little farfetched for Saudi women who were not allowed to be unveiled in the presence of unrelated males. How could a Saudi woman have the opportunity to "start anything"? It was easy! In the hospital, we occasionally had male psychology students doing clinical work at the same time that we had female social work students. Supervision was poor as neither the supervising social worker not the supervising psychologist were often on the floor where we all were. We other staff had little time or authority to reprimand these students for fraternizing against cultural mores. It was easy for them to slip off together. I frequently saw them walking down hallways together ostensibly discussing patients. If they learned to subvert the segregation that easily as students, they will certainly continue it as professionals. Even teachers, who really worked in a segregated system, had necessary meetings with their opposite sex counterparts and supervisors, which were opportunities for discussion which might lead to conversation, which might lead to assignations.

The work of women continues to be 'house work'. Even as they discussed their future professional careers, students emphasized the role of mother as the "natural" one for all women. One student, with great shame, admitted to me that she did not want to become pregnant and bear children. Beck and Keddie (1978) stated it this way:

> Women, valued as an exchange good, as being a procreator and a means of sexual pleasure, in relations between families and lineages, is devalued as a person. Her status in the politics of lineages makes of her, besides, a subject of continual anxiety. The boy does pose the same problems. He is both a threat and protection; he is destined to head a family, to regulate the relations between this family and other families, notably through the politics of marriages. He is not imprisoned in the 'natural' roles of sex and reproduction; he is politics and culture, and 'on him rests the order of the world! p 85.

Therefore, males can be expected to dominate the world of work and money in Saudi Arabia for some time to come. Yes, women could possess money, but in order to be employed she had to have either her father or husband's consent. It was difficult to make career choices and plans under those restrictions.

The careers that were legally open to Saudi women at that time were teacher, doctor, social worker, nurse, psychologist, secretary, domestic and librarian, all to be pursued in segregated situations. That did not leave leeway for career planning. The reader may note that each of the above mentioned possibilities had aspects that we commonly associate with wifeliness, nurture, motherhood and housework.

In the Work Force Reports, produced by the Central Department of Statistics in the Ministry of Finance and National Economy, women were not included, along with the unemployed. When reading these reports one would get the idea that there were no employed women as well as no unemployed people. And of course, both of the above are untrue.

One item which amused me from the *Labor and Workmen Law* (1981) referred to regulations of an infraction I saw daily:

> The employer must always and continuously enclose, within suitable protective guards all moving parts of power generators and transmission gears, as well as the dangerous parts of the machines, whether they are stationary or mobile, unless these parts are so designed or installed as to provide protection. He must also fence the manholes and all obstructions that may expose workmen to the dangers of falling or collision. *Article 131.*

79

I never saw a fenced manhole. They were left open and dangerous for months on end. No warning for pedestrians either, just constant vigilance. Gasoline engines for construction or street work stood unprotected on streets and walkways. As the beginning I thought it was just because they had not yet had time in their rush to industrialization to think of such things until I read the laws which were enacted but obviously not enforced when King Faisal, now deceased, signed them in 1969.

Another section which concerned me as an occupational therapist was Article 54 *Labor and Workmen Law*:

> Any employer who employs 50 or more workmen, and the nature of whose work allows him to employ disabled workmen who have been vocationally rehabilitated, shall employ such workmen to the extent of 2% of the total of his workmen...

In the Arabic version, it says 1% of the total workmen. It will probably be a long time until a disabled English speaking worker challenges this law, but when and if they do, the Arabic version will prevail. My experience as a therapist trying to help patients get work or return to their former jobs was that this law was not observed. The attitude was that the disabled person must have somehow gravely offended Allah. To be denied work was just punishment. The handicapped were seldom strong enough in their self-esteem to feel justified in advancing their own cause. Most refused to stand up on their own behalf and insist on retraining. One patient was successful in getting the hospital to train him and was later employed by the hospital, but he used his interpersonal persuasion skills rather than the labor court.

When the goal of governments is to keep unemployment down, one way to do it is to employ people in non-productive "paper-pushing" jobs. The Saudis carried this to an extreme in some cases. For example, in order for me to retrieve the 2500 riyals which at that time was the equivalent of American $700, housing deposit from the University Housing Office, it was necessary for me to visit seven different offices, three of those offices required two visits apiece, nine visits in all to get this refund. Seven signatures were required on a variety of papers despite the fact that I was able to produce my receipt for the original 2500 riyals.

I was so dismayed when I found during Ramadan, that two of those offices had closed half an hour early and left me waiting over the weekend to complete my transaction that I decided to give a little performance so they would remember not to do this again. I squeezed my tear glands until I was able to produce sufficient tears to accompany my statement "This is no way to treat a lady! A lady without a car, without a husband, who cannot come back again. It is very bad for the University to treat people like this!" It was a fruitless performance if measured in the riyals it produced. But Saudi men cannot tolerate a weeping female I discovered. None-the-less, I had to wait all weekend before getting my money. However, I will never know if that performance may have impressed them with the difficulty they put on their female workers.

REFERENCES:

Ali, Abdallah Yousef (1931) *The Quran*, Egypt.

"Arabian Nights in Miami" (April 26, 1982) *Newsweek.*

Beck, Lois & Keddie, Nikki (1978) *Women in the Muslim World*. Cambridge, MA: Harvard University Press.

Labor and Workmen Law , 3rd edition (1980).Government Security Press, Riyadh, 1401 H.

Miller, Jean Baker (1976) *Toward a New Psychology of Women*. Boston: Beacon Press.

Watt, W. Montgomery (1961). *Islam and the Integration of Society*. London: Routledge & Kegan Paul, Ltd.

Youssef, Nadi (1978) The status and fertility patterns of Muslim women, in *Women in the Muslim World* by Beck, L & Keddie, N. Cambridge, MA: Harvard University Press.

9
TRANSPORTATION

Sura XXII Verse 46
Do they not travel
Through the land, so that
Their hearts (and minds)
May thus learn wisdom
And their ears may
Thus learn to hear?
Truly it is not their eyes
That are blind, but their
Hearts which are
In their breasts.

Transportation in Saudi Arabia, for me, usually meant riding buses. Women did not drive. It was not that they were not allowed to drive. They were not issued driver's licenses.

The University gave all faculty of my rank five hundred riyals per month which was the equivalent of $147.00 as a transportation allowance. This was supposed to pay for whatever method we used - buses, taxis, private drivers, and shoes meant for walking. Men could buy cars and so could we, but we could not be licensed to drive them. Taxi drivers were quickly on my 'bad list' from my very first experience with one. In my journal of September 3, 1980,

I told about getting my new home furnishings purchased and back to the flat in a taxi, the first and last time I ever rode alone in a taxi:

> "I found what I wanted, a foam mattress, pillow and free standing coat rack. After making my deal, getting the mattress rolled, and the coat rack disassembled, two old men carried them down a long dark alley-way to the street where I hailed a taxi and bargained with him to drive me and my purchases back to the flat. The mattress which was one and one half meters by two meters went into the trunk. The two pieces of the coat rack and the pillow went on the back seat. And I had to sit in the front passenger seat. On the way, he put his hand on my knee three times. I said, "No, no!" Then I said it in Arabia, "La, la!" He said pointing to Mama's wedding ring on my left hand saying "Bebe, bebe, bebe?" "La, la!" I said. Then he grinned and kept saying "Bebe, bebe, bebe!" I wanted to sock him but was afraid of causing him to crash."

I got home safely from that one, but immediately I began to hear tales of women being driven out into the desert and raped, so I stopped all taxi riding unless someone else was with me. They do have a bloody lot of gall. One time, four women got into a cab together which meant one of us had to ride in the front passenger seat. The other three women climbed into the back seat thus leaving me to sit in the front. While driving, the driver reached over and touched my hand right in front of my three colleagues. Now he knew he was not supposed to do that. I just pulled my hand away and said emphatically, "La, la!" Some made the argument that these Bedouin men just off the desert just did not know the amenities. I felt that was a very weak argument, since Islam also had the 'golden rule'. They would not allow such treatment of their own women; in fact, three hundred fifty men went to jail in Riyadh in 1981 "for annoying women". These drivers knew when they were driving that they had the power to transport or destroy and that if a woman lashed out at them, she risked causing an accident; therefore they probably felt they could do what they liked. Additionally, it was actually against the law for a lone woman to take a taxi, so most women would find no protection in the courts under these circumstances.

One of my middle-aged Egyptian Muslim colleagues, who had already been working in Riyadh one year, was driven out to the desert and offered money and other inducements to participate in sexual activities. The driver continued until his tank was almost empty three hours later before he brought her back to town and swore her to secrecy. She wouldn't have wanted to report him anyway because of her own legal vulnerability for going alone and also foreigners disliked becoming involved with <u>any</u> Saudi in court. Only Saudis and Yemenis were allowed to drive taxis. Since it was an occupation in which literacy was not required, many taxi drivers were illiterate. It was no use having a destination written in Arabic for them. Often men who came to that occupation were not qualified for any other.

On one occasion, a fifty year old grey-haired American grandmother took a taxi down to the souq to meet a friend for shopping. Immediately after giving the driver her destination, she noticed that he was driving with one hand and masturbating with the other. She pretended not to notice and ignored him when he attempted to start a conversation. She paid and fled as soon as possible. After her shopping spree, she again hailed a cab which passed her by, then another also refused to take a lone woman and finally, feeling rather desperate, she got the third cab which she hailed to take her home. Once in the cab, still preoccupied with her purchases, she slowly came to the awareness that this was the same masturbating cab driver who brought her to the souq. He was still masturbating! And he became a little bolder in his conversation. He spoke about how bad off it was for men in Saudi Arabia. He was Yemeni. He said, "I've gotta have a woman. Any woman will do." This was bound to increase her self- image! And the grandmother responded in her best grandmotherly voice, "I know. It seems pretty bad but you'll be married soon and everything will be alright." Never mind how cool and collected she was she was scared!

But women did drive on occasion, though I never did. I frequently wanted to, especially when riding with a male whom I felt was a less competent driver than me. Californians tended to be quite smug about their driving skills and I included myself in that group. Some of the reports of women driving were Bedouin women, out away from the city, and young women dressed up as men driving within the city. I could not personally verify these reports, but several camping friends told of seeing women driving Toyota trucks across the desert.

Why was it that they did not want women to drive? Dawn Chatty (1978) had some theories in the concluding passage of the article "Changing Sex Roles in Bedouin Society";

> The shift from camel to truck transport has been a positive factor in the pastoral way of life, in general and in the maintenance of the family and lineage solidarity, in particular. The truck's use, however has affected men and women differently. The emotional attachment women once felt for the camel, has not been transferred to the truck. Though women now have

increased interaction with non-tribesmen, their access to tribal non-kinswomen has declined. Men, who did not appear to have an emotional attachment to the camel, now place a high value on the truck. This value is not simply based on economics; it also relates to the fact that the truck has become a focal point of male solidarity. p. 413.

And I think those same male views applied to cars. An interview with the marketing director of the bus company Saudi Arabian Public Transportation Company (SAPTCO) produced the following information. When busses first started running, they were originally intended for transportation of women, since women could not drive. But when the women's section was the front half of the bus was the women's section and men rode in back behind a screen, hardly any women rode, so it quickly became apparent that financially, it was not good business to reserve half of the bus for women when that section was almost empty. So they put women in the back over the engine and bumpy back axle with only one window to cool the section. There were eight places for sitting and three for standing, however, on more than one occasion, I rode with fifteen other women in that tiny space. One of my colleagues from the University believed her miscarriage to have been induced by the bumpiness and heat. This was not so far fetched an idea as one might think. Some drivers were very rough.

One of the problems the marketing director found most difficult was providing drivers. Initially, they had been mostly Filipinos and Thais who were trained in desert camps, then brought to the city to drive. That worked well until the Ministry of Labor directed the company to have at least forty percent Saudi drivers/trainees. The company attempted to comply with that edict, but found that the Saudi drivers did not show up for work, or did not drive on time schedules. So they reassigned expatriate drivers to the routes.

Another story he told was of a time when thousands of people arrived at the bus station to take buses to Mecca to perform the *haj*, or pilgrimage. But only one driver showed up. So they had to take some of their non-Muslim expatriate drivers off the city routes and send them to Mecca with the hajies. He said they had far surpassed the numbers of riders they had originally anticipated, having had two hundred thousand already by June 1982. I wondered if the non-Muslim drivers were allowed within the sacred precincts.

Initially, during my first few months when the front of the bus was for women, the driver took my fare of one riyal or about thirty five cents. There was a Masonite floor to ceiling barrier between the front and back halves. The conductor was in the back half for men. A door for each section was clearly marked in English and Arabic 'For Women Only' and 'For Men Only'. But so few women rode the bus, that within my first month I was beginning to see the gradual change to the tiny walled off back section for women. So many more men rode the bus that I could not blame them for this good business move. They did not use a conductor in the back for the women as there was no room for him or her to stand and of course a man would not be allowed into the women's section anyway, except the essential driver. This also cut their staff requirements by half. They had increased the total seating capacity for males to eighty percent of the bus. Unfortunately, it consigned me to the back where there was one long seat and then the two person seat by the window. The entrance stairs was where the seat would have been on the other side. The buses were not air-conditioned. It really became a hot-box back there sometimes. The handrails were too hot to touch.

Then in the last third of my first year, they started introducing double decker buses. This meant a new adjustment for us women. Now we had to enter through the exit the men used from the second level. It was in the middle and went to the stairs to the second level. The women's section was the back third of the bottom level. The door into that section was bout four feet high so we had to duck to enter. There was a projection from the stairway right inside that frequently knocked me and others in the head. We could not stand upright in that back section of the double decker although there were now plenty of seats, enough for twenty. But these enormous vehicles traveled only the busiest routes which were not to the University or the hospital where I worked some hours each week, so I was not often forced into crawling into that type of bus.

Sura IV Verse 101

When ye travel
Through the earth,
If ye shorten your prayers,
For fear the Unbelievers
May attack you:
For the Unbelievers are
Unto you open enemies . . .
Take all precautions . . .
For the Unbelievers
God hath prepared
A humiliating punishment.

The needs of travel and transportation appeared not to have any effect on lengths of prayer times in Saudi Arabia. "Petrol" stations as most expatriates called gas stations or "benzene" stations as Arabs called them carefully observed the closing times for prayers. By the end of prayer time, usually there would be a line of impatient drivers waiting in a line out into the street. Gasoline was cheap. At home in California in the summer of 1981, gasoline cost $1.35 for unleaded for my VW Rabbit. In Saudi Arabia I never saw anyone pay more than fifteen riyals to fill the tank of a big fat American car. That meant that a tank of gasoline cost about $4.50. It was available and easily accessible at all times except during prayer.

One of the problems for Saudi drivers, although they did not consider it a problem, was the *ghutra* or the head-cloth. It prevented peripheral vision. Once, the bus on which I was riding to school slowly pulled away from the bus stop and an old Saudi man driving his daughter to school pulled right in front of the bus because his *ghutra* blocked his view of the bus. His brand new Mercedes got a smashed door and window, but his daughter in the back seat, surprisingly was OK.

Driving traffic had priority over any walking traffic as evidenced by the freedom with which cars pulled up and parked on sidewalks. Occasionally, there would be an attempt to discourage his practice. The police would put a giant clamp on the rear wheel so that the car could not be driven until the police unlocked it. However, the attitude of the government traffic people was ambivalent. A consultant on mobility training for the blind went during "Traffic Safety Week" to call on the Minister. He had a list of ten things that would allow the blind to have greater independent mobility within the city. One of these was "no parking on the sidewalks". The Minister's response was, "But where would people park?"

Women in automobiles were expected to sit in the back seat. In fact we always heard rumors of how we would be jailed if we were found in the front seat of a car with a man to whom we were not married. I had no first hand knowledge of such police action because the only time I was ever in a car stopped by the police, was during a camping trip when two four-wheel drive vehicles were caravanning and I was in the front seat of the second vehicle. The married British couple in the first vehicle sweet talked us both through the village checkpoint. So they never even asked for my papers.

One rumor I heard which scared me for a time was about a woman whose husband was sent to Jeddah for a few days on business. A male neighbor from the same compound drove her to do her shopping and on the way they had a minor traffic violation. When the police saw from their papers that they were not married, they took the man to jail and the woman to the hospital where I worked and gave her a vaginal examination. Semen was found in her vagina because her husband had been with her during the night only leaving that morning. The man was judged guilty and continued in jail. She was sent out of the country immediately, or so the story went. After a scary story like that, I was apt to tell my dates that I would sit in the back seat, until my anxiety level could tolerate illegally sitting in the front beside them again. If we both looked American or European, the risk was small.

When cars with Saudi Arabian license plates crossed the border into another country, they were required to relinquish their Saudi plates. They could be reclaimed on reentry. A driver who had this experience asked the border guards why they did that. A guard replied, "It keeps people from shaming Saudi Arabia. If their driving or behavior was bad, it would not reflect on the Kingdom." If this was indeed the reason, it was typical of the royal family's attempts to keep the rest of the world from knowing that the custodians of the Islamic Holy Places were not saints.

The Arabs delightfully decorated their jeeps, trucks and lorries. They embellished the cabs and top of the side-gates with wrought iron. It was then painted in a pattern of bright colors somewhat like a carpet design. The cargo areas of the huge Mercedes Benz "lorries" were decorated in a wide variety of colorful geometrics. And along the gas tanks, tool boxes and containers under the lower edge of the cargo section were painted stylized scenes of sailboats on lakes and cottages set in meadows by ponds. These desert truck drivers carried their bit of water and grass along with them in the pictures.

One of the travel adventures I had inside Saudi Arabia was a trip by train from Riyadh to Dammam with three friends in January 1981. I describe it thusly in my journal:

> "Well, the first adventure took place on the day before we were to leave. We knew we had to buy tickets the day before, but no other information could we get from three travel agents. Three of us took a taxi to the train station to inquire. A handsome young English speaking Pakistani told us we could come back between four and ten pm to buy tickets for tomorrow. I asked, just to clear things up, if we had to have a man buy our tickets, since we had heard such rumors. He said, "No," and also "No" to a question about a man to accompany us. So we relaxed and took a taxi home.
>
> So at eight in the evening, a friend drove us back to the station. We had all the *igamas,* our work visas and money for our four tickets. We went boldly up to the ticket window and another Pakistani looked at our *igamas* for a minute and asked, "All women?" "Yes", we replied. "Can't do it. Have to have a man accompany you." Well, we were astonished since we had

asked directly in relation to this in the morning. We told him of our morning inquiry but he stood firm. So I said in an aside to my male friend "Buy a ticket!" So he went to his car and got his *igama*. It was in his car as he dast not drive without it in case of accident; in fact none of us foreigners should be outside our buildings without them. I gave him the money to buy a ticket for him. We just planned and hoped to walk on the train next morning, without him since he had to work.

Our train was to leave at 8 am, they had said. My friend picked us up at 7 am and took us to the station before going to his work. We waited in the ladies waiting room since they are always segregated. One friend used the restroom. I did not but she reported that it was the Eastern *hammam* or hole in the floor. That's why I did not try it. I hate that kind and frequently they are the only ones available.

So the train loaded about 7:50 am. Two Saudi women in veils had joined us in the waiting room. So we just got into line behind them and went right into our first class car. But it had a Western toilet. Hurrah! The four of us sat facing each other. It stopped about every hour at small villages. It was just sand hills and more sand hills. We had brought our lunch. Near the end of the journey, three of us went to the dining car to try to get coffee, but the soldier stopped us before we had gone that far and motioned to us to go into this little green curtained booth, so we did. We did not bother to close the curtain so he came over and thrust it shut. My two companions lit up cigarettes so in a moment, a hand came in and put down an ashtray. The waiter stuck his head through to get our orders and brought them back. Well, it was not too nice being shut up in a one meter by one meter curtained cubicle so we did not stay long. When we finally got to the village station near ARAMCO and got off, we saw a list of railroad rules on the wall, the first of which read "It is absolutely unacceptable for women to travel by train without being accompanied by a *maharram*," which is a father, a brother, a son or a husband. I read on down to find we had broken another rule because we were forbidden to carry any meat and we had chicken and roast beef with us. But we did not write on the backs of our chairs which was also forbidden so perhaps we redeemed ourselves.

For a long time I puzzled over why carrying meat was forbidden, but it finally occurred to me that meat thus carried could not be fresh meat. Sura V Verse 4 starts out "Forbidden to you are: dead meat . . ." and obviously if we carried it in our bags it was getting deader and deader.

Now with the airline, I was allowed to just buy my ticket at the travel agency and go to the airport and get on the plane... as long as the destination was within the Kingdom. Upon leaving the Kingdom, the process became much more arduous. When the University gave me my travel voucher, I would take it to the travel agent who had made my reservations. He would give me my itinerary and perhaps the computer number of my ticket. Then I would take the bus to the airport, and go to the Saudia Airlines office. I would stand in line in order to get my name on a waiting list which was usually one page long. Usually, I was the only woman in sight. Then I would try to find a seat on one of the nine three-seat benches. Men almost never offered their seats, nor would I have expected it at home in the USA, but in Saudi Arabia where I was not allowed to drive I hoped always to be treated as the fragile creature they thought me to be, but no, no seats were offered. Every half hour or so I would go up to the ticket desk where the agent was consulting the computer to see how far down the list they had moved. Once, I timed it and each client took approximately forty minutes. Many of the people on the list left in frustration so the agents moved along more quickly than those figures would indicate. Also three agents were working from the same waiting list passing it back and forth, as well as passing back and forth the books containing the time tables. These paper exchanges took lots of time and distracted the agents who seemed to have remarkably short attention spans. The distractions added to the time involved. Finally, it would be my turn. Government vouchers had so many restrictions that any deviation from the exact destination printed on the paper involved consulting the supervisor, and then the manager on the second floor. But I was lucky in the case in which my destination was listed as Long Beach and I had requested to go to Los Angeles International Airport instead because Long Beach handled only inter-California flights. The agent consulted only the book, not the supervisor. This took only ten minutes including distractions. But when I wanted to stop at Cairo instead of flying directly to Los Angeles, via New York, it was necessary to consult the supervisor who referred it to the manager, who was in a half-hour meeting, I was informed. I was requested to sit and wait. Finally after standing prominently by the supervisor's desk for several minutes, he went upstairs and in a few minutes motioned for me to come up. I was shown to an office where six people were already waiting and the manager was leafing through the regulation book. After about five minutes he looked up and gave some sort of answer to the man in front of me. Then he indicated his attention to me by a glance. I offered the others who had been waiting longer to go first, but in the usual fashion, he did not want a woman in his office any longer than necessary, so he served me first to get me out. I was told emphatically two times, that I could not stop in the Middle East on a government voucher. In my original interview, I was given propaganda about exotic travel opportunities. So I looked crest fallen and on the point of tears, so he said "OK, but you will have to go to Rome and Paris, too." Such hard luck! I said "Anyplace after Cairo!" So he wrote a note to that effect on the paper I had already spent another hour obtaining from the University which already authorized me to stop in Cairo. Back downstairs, it took me only another forty minutes to get the actual ticket in my hand. Then two days before departure, it was necessary for me to take my passport marked with the exit visa to the travel agent who would then send it to the airport for me to confirm my reservation and I suppose to make some sort of check that I was not wanted by the police. I was never told this exactly but Filipino health care workers who were employed by the Ministry of Health did indeed go through a police check before being allowed to leave, even on holiday.

At Christmas time, a daughter of friends was arriving by plane for her holiday with her parents. They arrived at the airport and the mother went in to collect the teenager while the father parked the car. When the mother and daughter attempted to leave the arrival lounge, the official stopped them and informed them that the father of the girl would have to accompany her out of the airport. My friend said in her best imperious voice "But I am her mother!" The official coldly responded with "A man is required to accompany young females." So my friend was required to go out, find her husband and bring him back before they could extricate their daughter from the clutches of the airline.

Saudi women are so disadvantaged in the realm of travel from my viewpoint. They cannot buy airline tickets, train tickets, get visas or drive cars. Unless some loving male wants to do those things for them, they are stuck.

REFERENCES:

Ali, Abdallah Yousef (1931) *The Quran*, Egypt.

Beck, Lois & Keddie, Nikki (1978) *Women in the Muslim World*. Cambridge, MA: Harvard University Press.

Chatty, Dawn (1978) Changing sex roles in Bedouin society in Syria and Lebanon in *Women in the Muslim World* by Beck, L & Keddie N. Cambridge MA: Harvard University Press.

Hall, Edward T. (1973) *The Silent Language*, New York: Anchor Books.

10

COMMUNICATION

❦

Sura IX Verse 79
Those who slander such
Of the Believers as give themselves
Freely to (deeds of) charity,
As well as such as can find
Nothing to give except
The fruits of their labour, - - -
And throw ridicule on them,
God will throw back their ridicule on them:
And they shall have a grievous penalty.

I have certainly tried not to slander in this book. When it was a rumor, I have reported it as a rumor, but when it happened to me, it became a fact, reported herein as such. Edward Hall (1979) the American writer on body language described the Arab culture as "high context" compared to our which called "low context". In a "high context" culture, the content of a communication is much less important than the circumstances and actions surrounding the message. A "low context" situation is one in which we Americans frequently operate. We expect to deal with many people on things without becoming emotionally involved; when we walk into an office, we state our business and expect a brief answer or response. When an Arab walks into an office, he or she expects to spend several minutes with amenities regarding both the other party's health, family and describing their own health. Usually, at the first meeting, I learned through my own experience, that the only <u>real</u> piece of information exchanged is the reason for establishing contact. Then another meeting or two may be required before a person can begin to accomplish the task for which the original contact was made. My own particular experience was when I wanted to begin to do some research which was one of my objectives mentioned in my interview in Houston. On my first visit to my superior, I stated the reason for coming and his initial response was "No, no, you haven't lived in Saudi Arabia long enough to be qualified to do research." At this time, I had been there three and one half months. But by the end of the discussion he was willing for me to come back another day and discuss it again. I did so. Finally, after the third visit, I had his permission to begin research. It was only months later I learned that I did not even need his permission for that particular research. He, of course, never told me that. He allowed me to go through the whole sequence of superfluous meetings. But the context of the communication was more important than the information, that I was asking his permission.

Sura XXX Verse 22

And among His Signs
Is the creation of the heavens
And the earth, and the variations
In your languages
And your colors: verily
In that are Signs
For those who know.

In 1982, English was the second language of Saudi Arabia. The historical association with Great Britain through her domination of the Arabian/Persian Gulf area during the Victorian era played a great role in that development. Current atlases call it simply "The Gulf". But in 1982, the Arabs called it the Arabian Gulf and the Iranians and most maps called it the Persian Gulf. Now that English has become the language of science and computers; since the Saudis have valiantly tried to bring science and technology to their country, English is spoken almost everywhere in the country. The Saudi students learned English before they could enter any medical or allied health program. We gave our lectures in English. Most medical literature, medical vocabulary and terms were English. It was felt that English was necessary in order to encourage our students to keep current in their professions. Further employment at the conclusion of university training would most surely involve supervision of foreigners who also spoke more English than Arabic. This was surely true of the Filipinos, the Koreans, the Pakistanis, the English, Australians and Americans already in the Kingdom.

Since there were an estimated three million foreigners working in Saudi Arabia, one would guess that the postal system took quite a load compared to what might have been required for only the estimated five million Saudis. Letters within the Kingdom cost twenty *halalas* which was about nine cents. The letters to the USA cost one riyal and twenty *halalas* or approximately forty three cents. There was no mail delivery. Each recipient must have a post office box. In the University, each college had its own individual box. A man went from each college to pick up the mail. It was then distributed. Letters which came to me usually took two to five days longer to get to me than the letters which I sent back to the USA. Frequently, the mail man from our office just did not go and pick it up. The usual thing was for him to pick it up only three times per week. So when a telex or cable arrived, it would not be delivered immediately, but could lie in the box over the weekend. And our mail could lie in the men's office another day or two before they decided to forward it to the women's office.

Once, inadvertently, I made the mistake of trying to enter the section of the post office where the post boxes were and an ancient Saudi man yelled at me and waved his arms. Some other Arabic/English speaking foreigner took pity on me when he saw the bewildered expression on my face. "The old man is say, 'Women are not allowed'". Later I came to know the reason. Women were not allowed to have post boxes, and therefore, not allowed to enter that section of the post office. Men controlled women's access to written communication, too.

At the telephone company, there were segregated waiting rooms for women, but not at the post office. I wondered whether the new post office scheduled to open shortly after my departure would have separate women's waiting rooms and service windows. There were an ever increasing number of single foreign women who mailed their own letters and bought their own stamps.

In Houston, I was given the impression that there were several hours of English television each evening. However, upon arrival in Riyadh, I found that in reality, the English news was all I could regularly expect. I described it thus in my journal:

> The news this evening is the usual concentration on the royal males with King Hussein coming to visit, the various royalty of other Muslim countries coming to make *haj* and getting greeted by King Khalid and his various princes. This sort of

thing takes up about eight minutes of the fifteen minutes of English news each evening. Then the remainder told how many were reported wounded and killed in Iraq and Iran. The news here is so insular, provincial and controlled. I guess "good news" is one of the things I miss most acutely.

After I had been there almost two years and got to know some 'old timers', they said that indeed, there used to be several hours of English programming each evening. But gradually, as fear of Iran, the Shiites and revolution increased after the attempted Mecca takeover of 1979, entertainment on television decreased, leaving mostly only religious programming. This consisted of question and answer competitions between male students about lectures and prayers. There was usually an English cartoon in the late afternoon, but only on two occasions was I able to see an English language program on TV for other than children. They were interested in having their children learn the second language, English.

Telephone systems were still very much in the process of development despite what Robert Lacy (1981) reported in the book *The Kingdom*. The main foreign company involved with assisting and training Saudis was Canadian Bell Telephone. They claimed to have the biggest living compound in the Kingdom after ARAMCO. A visit there put me in agreement with them. There were blocks and blocks of villas and flats and single men's dormitories. A movie theater , which is the only one I ever saw in the Kingdom, a small hospital, several swimming pools, tennis courts, children's play grounds, offices, etc were there. It was a small city, all in tones of sandy-beige. With the Saudi's fears of large assemblies, I wondered how Canadian Bell Telephone was ever able to convince them to house so many foreigners together. Some young male Saudi trainees lived in a dormitory within the compound but were restricted to a certain area because if they were allowed to, they would have spent their entire time at the family swimming pool watching the women, my informant told me.

Telephone trouble punctuated my time there. I had a series of stories in my journal which I called Telephone Tribulation Tales:

Tale One, October 1980

When I came here I expected very little. Almost everything is better than I imagined it from my snug house in Long Beach. I never expected a telephone. I would have felt that one in the lobby was a blessing. However, our apartment had two telephones, one was an outside line and one was internal for the various apartments and the hospital. Everything went well for the first two weeks. Then suddenly, one day a tape recording in both English and Arabia said, "This is a recording. Your telephone service has been disconnected for non-payment; please see your nearest payment office." Well, my flat-mate had come back from vacation low on funds to find a horrible phone bill. She did not pay it immediately to the University who collected the money from everybody in the building, so they were late in paying her bill. So our phone was cut off. I felt this was her responsibility so just let her take care of getting it back on. She visited the University Hospital offices. They said they would pay it since she had already paid them. A week went by and the phone was still off. So we both went over to the office. "We have paid the money," they said. Another three days went by and no change occurred so I went to the office alone. Three days later with still no change, I went to the office again. Attempts were made by the office personnel, within my presence to call the telephone company. A few days later, my flat-mate went again. Finally, about a week ago, we got a dial tone and assumed it was OK. After two days with no incoming calls, we asked someone to call us. Impossible! We could call out but nobody could call in. So my flat-mate called the telephone repair service directly. I tried to call them also but got busy signals for hours on end. Finally she made contact and they said they would be out to check on it. Nothing! So we called two days later. And yesterday after a trip to the souq, the damned thing was giving us the "Your service has been disconnected for non-payment" recording again. Extremely frustrated after one month of this, we decided to walk to our nearest telephone office, where, after talking to three different men, we were directed to another office farther down the road. There we were again directed to another office even farther down the road. At the fourth building, we found the V.I.P. Office which had closed about fifteen minutes before. I was in the process of writing a desperate note when a cleaning man opened the door next to it and we saw a Westerner inside. So we went in, despite the office being closed and told our sad story again. The two Canadian men gave us coffee and told us to get our original bill from the University and bring it for them to see. I made my story even more poignant by saying that all the other University teachers were taking trips so I would be left alone without transportation or communication. I thought hopefully that my flat-mate would be able to get a copy of the original bill on that day and we could take it back down to the office and get the damned telephone turned on.

Four days later, the telephone was back on. We learned in the process of solving this problem that the telephone company was moving from one office to another and thus lost our bill in between. That was before we visited the V.I.P. Office. At that office they had said something about somebody being in the midst of some negotiations with somebody and a lot of peoples' phones had been cut off. And then, they also said something about the University not paying a bill for five thousand riyals and maybe that was why we were having this problem. However, nobody else in our building was having that problem and our telephones were all numbered consecutively. So who knew why? These sorts of occurrences seemed to me to come from a kind of "frontier mentality" where there are just so many problems to solve that one can hardly decide which one to concentrate on as well as how to solve it.

Tale Two, September 10, 1981

Today, I am supposed to get a telephone in my new flat. I've been without one ever since I moved to this building in April. When we first moved, the housing office told us there were no cables to the building and that the owner of the building from whom the University had leased it had been asked to apply for telephone service but the University could not require him to do that.

Then we began to notice that people around us had telephones, were getting telephones; the phone truck was often sitting in front of our building. Millie walked the twenty or so blocks to the phone company in the 120'F heat and got applications for the three of us women who live in this building. So I filled mine out and left the space blank that was for the required Saudi male sponsor who had to sign saying he would pay my bill if I left the country without paying. And then I found out that our dean who was supposed to sign for us had refused. So there we three were, not supposed to talk to men, especially Saudi men whom we might lure away from Islam, yet we could not get a telephone with out the help of one. So we just let it go since none of us knew whether we wanted to return to such a place where we were placed in such a position.

I came back on August 22, and Judy returned a week later but Millie did not return. Well, last Saturday which is like Monday to me, Judy went to the housing office and got a paper from them introducing her to the phone company and saying what her rank within the University is. So the next day, I did not go to the hospital as I had planned, but instead went to housing to get such a paper for myself, then went on to the telephone company. We went to the VIP Office where I had been helped before. Well, they looked at our papers and filled out some more papers and were just about to say OK when they saw that we did not have the signature of a Saudi male sponsor. With great regret, this sweet young Scot sent us back five miles to the housing office but on the way he sent the telephone surveyor, because they had given us maps to fill out with directions to our flat. They felt ours were not clear enough. Judy did not want to mess with the surveyor, because she was so mad with the University that she wanted to go straight there, but I knew if they were sending the surveyor, we'd better go with him since another friend had missed the telephone men twice when they came to install his because there were no street numbers and few street names, essentially no street addresses. So the surveyor came in and immediately verified where the cables were and had been for several years, we learned and that there were vacant cables for us and that each flat already had an outlet, something I had overlooked since it was behind a heavy piece of furniture. So the surveyor nicely took us and dropped us back at the University Housing Office. We went in to say that the piece of paper they had given us was no good as the telephone company wanted someone from the University to sign a new form that they had given us and get the University stamp on it. Well, all five of the men in the housing office said "No, no, no! We never do that!" Judy started to tell them how we could not get a phone and how long we had been trying. I started telling then what a bind it put us in, not supposed to be talking to Saudi men yet requiring us to solicit a Saudi sponsor and breaking the Islamic Shariah law. While I was saying that, fortunately Judy started crying and just got up and was at the door before I realized what had happened. So in a moment I followed her thoroughly disgusted with this situation but not with her tears. We just got to the bottom of the Administration Building steps when we heard "Judy! Judy!" It was Hameed who is married to an American. He had followed us out of the housing office. He told us we must not leave but go and see the Vice Rector. Judy did not want to since her eyes were all red, but finally, Hameed and I convinced her to come with me to try. I told her I'd do all the talking but when we got there, she just couldn't keep quiet and started telling the Vice Rector herself, which was fine with me. I'm not too coherent when I am angry anyway.

The Vice Rector's glass covered desk is bigger than my bathroom in Long Beach. His office is bigger than my whole house. He listened, took a piece of paper and wrote a note, clipped it to our empty telephone forms and told us to see the head of personnel. So we went out and asked the Vice Rector's secretary who is always a male, how to find the personnel director's office. He told us to wait as he was on his way there that very moment. A few moments later, a non-English speaking Saudi man came in and with some translation help from the secretary, sent us to yet another office floor below.

That was the office of a darling Egyptian translator. After another fifteen minutes of him trying to tell us we had to get a Saudi sponsor again, we persuaded him to read the note from the Vice Rector which said in Arabia that we were to have a special dispensation and the University was to sign for us, a thing they had ceased to do a few years ago. Apparently a bunch of expatriate teachers had gone off leaving big overseas phone bills. So the translator said,

"Come back tonight at seven o'clock and it will be done." So we went home and rested after all that.

So we walked the fifteen blocks there at seven o'clock to find out that he meant they would DO it at seven o'clock. When we walked in, this little Saudi went in and out of the translator's office five times, then led us across the parking lot to another office building to sign and get a University stamp as the telephone man had insisted. While we were in the translator's office, the little Saudi man insisted that we be told twice that this was an exception and that we must keep it a secret.

Anyway, so here it is, only three days later, and we are getting our telephone. So I must await them here all day. This is no different from General Telephone in Long Beach. Never mind, I shall just be glad to have a phone. How can I carry on an active social life here where social life is forbidden if I don't have a telephone to tell dates when and where to pick me up? I ask you now!

Poor Judy waited yet another two weeks because the line into her flat was bad. The telephone required that she find and pay someone to fix it before they would install her phone.

Tale Three

On about June 5, 1982, I got a form from the University Administration Office to get filled in so I could make a final check out to the University and get my back pay. I did this when I went there to get my ticket voucher verified for Cairo. The male secretary in the men's office of our college told me if I gave fifty riyals or about fifteen dollars to the little errand man, he would go and get it filled out for me, so I did since the form had about fifty five squares that needed filling and the temperature was near 130'F daily and he had a car. I did not. The next Saturday morning when we started our work week, the secretary informed me by telephone that I must get my final telephone bill so the square on the form about no outstanding bills could be signed off. So immediately, that day, I began to call the telephone company in order for it to be taken care of. I called the 'accounts office" listed in the telephone book. They referred me to another number where I was unable to get an answer. So I called the VIP Office through which Judy and I had originally gotten our phones. They told me to call another number and if I got no satisfaction, then to call them back. So I followed their instructions. The man who answered at the next number said I should bring a letter to his office requesting that my telephone service be cancelled. So I did. The same day King Khalid died. I was afraid the office would not be open because the whole country went into several days of official mourning. But the man was there. He read my letter, told me I could not use the word "discontinue" so I amended it with a pen as instructed to "cancel". Discontinue meant to them that I was only going away on holiday, not permanently. Whose language is this anyway, I thought petulantly.

Then he took my money and gave me a "semi-final" bill. He told me to call another number in order to find out how to get my "last account". So I went right home on the bus in 120'F heat and did that. I called. They told me to come on Thursday which is like our Saturday, in the morning to pick up my "last account" any time after seven am. I had plans on that Thursday to visit one of the rare "farms" with some friends. I verified with them that we would not leave until eight am so I could have time to pick up my "last account". On Wednesday afternoon, I called the number to make sure my bill would be ready and got a tape recording which said, "This office will be closed and will be open eight to twelve on Thursday." That meant that they would not be there before I left for the farm. In the morning I called the same number again, as it was the one where they had told me to come after seven am. The same recording - so I went off to the farm.

On Saturday morning, I went to the telephone office hoping at last to pick up my "last account" where I had previously taken my letter requesting "cancellation". I found another man in the manager's seat and my young man from my first visit on the supplicant side of the desk. As soon as I arrived, my young man told the man in the manager's seat in Arabic why I was there. All the men got up and changed chairs and the two who previously occupied the manager's chair left and I was facing a third new "manager". He picked up the telephone and called upstairs and asked for my "final account". He wrote my number in Arabic numerals on another paper and gave it to a young boy and instructed him to go away and get something. Then he indicated to me to sit and wait. I did. After perhaps five minutes, he got out a form and filled it in in Arabic, then told me to take this form with my telephone to the office in my area of Jareer Street and they would give me my "final account". So I ran out, jumped on the bus, jumped off the bus, ran into my flat, took a long drink of water, unplugged the phone, put it in a plastic bag, ran out and across the street, jumped on the bus, and took the telephone and paper to the office he had indicated. I walked into the "Ladies Waiting Room". I was the only customer on this side. I walked up to the young man and told him I had come to turn in my telephone as instructed at the "subscription office" on Sitteen Street. He smiled, looked at the paper, looked at the telephone and said, "Not working?"

"No," I said. "I'm turning it in. I'm leaving."

"Oh, but this is not the office where you turn in telephones," he said.

"But," I said, "They told me to bring it here."

He said, "Well, you have to take it to the Al-Ambra Building by National Hospital. Do you know where that is?"

I decided it was a good time to play dumb, so I said, "No."

And he started to give me directions. Then I said, "Can I walk there?"

"Don't you have a car?" he asked incredulously.

"No," I replied in a long suffering voice, "But couldn't one of these repair men that is walking around here take me there? It is just so hot. And I've already taken the bus from the University to the Sitteen Street Office. From there back to my flat to pick up the telephone and then another bus here and it is so hot."

"So," he said, "I'll take you." What a nice man! He insisted that I sit in the front seat beside him because his car had bucket seats and only two doors. And weak air-conditioning! So we went to the building where he had intended to direct me. He asked me to sit in the car while he went in to see where to take the phone. He also asked me to turn off the engine if the temperature gauge began to read "too hot." The irony of this request and them not letting me drive made me laugh. So I did as he requested and pretty soon he came out saying that this was not the right office. I thought "and you planned to send me there". So we went back to the Sitteen Street Subscription Office from where I had originally started. He instructed me to sit in the waiting area while he went back to the manager's office. Pretty soon he came out with the papers I had given him, my "semi-final" bill, the copy of my request for cessation of service, and the letter to accompany the telephone to be handed in. And he said he needed a photocopy of my *igama* so we went up to the fourth floor for photocopying. Then we went back to the ground floor to give all my papers in since they apparently could not find the original of my letter requesting cancellation of services. After a wait of about ten minutes, I was handed a three inch by three inch note pad sheet with a stamp and some Arabic writing on it. My guide explained that the note said my service would be cut off in four days, and to call in four days to verify the cut off. I reminded him that since they now had my telephone, it would be hard for me to call.

"Oh, yes" he said comprehending.

Then I asked for my original "semi-final" bill back and the photocopy of my letter but he said, "Everything is *halas*, OK, finished!"

So then I asked him to please write on the small square of paper that my bill was paid. So he did. And for all my trouble, I ended up with a small square of paper on which was my proof that I had paid up and was entitled to my salary before leaving the Kingdom. So we went out to his car with my guide stopping only twice to kiss other men on both cheeks. He insisted on driving me across town to the Women's University. What a nice man! On the way, he told me about his wife and mother. Really, he was delightful!

But I did find it incredible how difficult it was to get my telephone service stopped and the bill marked PAID.

One week later, on the day before I was scheduled to leave; I went to our college administrative assistant to collect my last month's pay. As I sat discussing it with him in the high context fashion described by Edward Hall, another employee walked in with a handful of telephone bills, one of which was mine. "But I paid my bill two weeks ago. You have a photocopy of it."

And sure enough there on the administrative assistant's desk lay the photocopy of my "semi-final" bill marked paid. But they were still skeptical that I had paid my bill. I was so upset that this subject had come up again that I neglected to look at the amount myself. I asked them how much it was.

They said "Two thousand twenty-one riyals."

"What?" I said unbelievingly, "Almost six hundred and fifty dollars."

Well I looked later and saw that it was really only two hundred and twelve riyals. They had just mixed up the hundreds and thousands in their infrequent use of the English language. But then, I remembered that the amount I had paid was exactly the same amount as it said on the bill, the one they had refused to give back to me at the telephone office saying "Everything is finished!!" and that I would not need it any more, just use the bit of paper instead. So I called up the VIP Office and told the man my circumstances. The Englishman said, "You really screwed up, didn't you?"

"What, me screwed up?" I was furious. It's their system.

"You should have insisted on getting your bill back," he said. Well, I don't know what you do if they refuse to give the bill back. Whose mistake is it anyway? I was furious. So then he told me to tell my office to call the billing office to confirm that my bill was paid. They did. I finally received my last month's pay one hour before I was supposed to go to airport to make my final exit.

Attempts at modern communication systems were vast, including a satellite system which accompanied the king into the desert when he went camping and hunting. That required a small army of special communication vehicles. But on a smaller scale, communication seemed to follow the simple rules of the Bedouin. Because the press was rigidly controlled and censored, information was passed through gossip. In pre-technology times, the best way to get information had been from others who visited your tent or by going and visiting other tents. So sometimes the news or gossip was months or even a year old before one heard it. In the University there seemed very little attempt at organized dissemination of information. We would not be given a specific date upon which a certain holiday would start, instead just a rather general idea. So a few days before the Western faculty expected the beginning of the holiday to start, the Arabic students and faculty would just disappear from the scene. This same blurring of time limits occurred at the uptake of classes as well.

Censorship in newspapers, books and magazines was both comical and frustrating. If any part of a woman's body beneath the neck, except hands and feet, showed in a photograph, the censor covered the offending expanse of flesh with black felt tip pen. If there was an article in the *International Herald Tribune* that expressed views unacceptable to the censor, the column might be clipped out or the whole page removed. Liquor and cigarette advertisements were torn out of magazines, never mind what was on the other side of the page. Any article about Saudi Arabia which was not entirely favorable would probably never have passed the censor. Cookbooks had pork recipes torn out. It was a great mystery game to try to figure out what had been removed or covered from any periodical I bought. The name Israel would most surely be blacked out.

Such a system encouraged rumor, when specific information was lacking. Sometimes the rumors would start from the stories that our Arabic speaking colleagues reported to us from the Arabic language newspapers, a lot of which never got into the English language newspapers.

REFERENCES:

Ali, Abdallah Yousef (1931) *The Quran*, Egypt.

Hall, Edward T. (1973) *The Silent Language*, New York: Anchor Books.

Hall, Edward (August, 1979) "Learning the Arabs' Silent Language". *Psychology Today.*

Lacey, Robert C. (1981) *The Kingdom.* New York: Harcourt Brace and Jovanovich, Inc.

11

GOVERNMENT

Historically, most Arabic Peninsula governments had been tribal with just one "headman" apiece until Abdul-Aziz ibn Saud conquered the peninsula starting in 1902. Predating that, the head men took turns toppling one another. However, since the 1902 unification date, the sons of the first king, Abdul-Aziz ibn Saud, have continued as rulers. In the late fifties, the Council of Ministers was started informally. By the nineteen-seventies it had solidified its role and function. It was made up mostly of princes, but there were a few commoners, too. They would draft decrees and submit them to the King for approval. The King held regularly scheduled weekly sessions when commoners could approach him in the royal audience hall to plead various causes. These ranged from appeals about sentences from the Islamic court to money for medical rehabilitation in Great Britain.

Sura III Verse 104
Let there arise out of you
A band of people
Inviting to all that is good,
Enjoining what is right,
And forbidding what is wrong:
They are the ones
To attain felicity.

Surely King Abdul-Aziz ibn Saud had felt he was bringing this injunction in that Sura to pass. His family had a history of purification of the Islamic holy places by destroying forbidden idols. There is very little in the Koran directly referring to government or how to govern, for in the days of the Prophet, most tribes were governed by the local tribal chieftain and his long suit was strength and craftiness. And so it continued as demonstrated by the way in which fealty was sworn to King Fahad upon his taking over power from is deceased brother, Khalid on June 13, 1982. In each province, the individual male citizens of every tribe came to the various provincial capitols too swear to the governor loyalty to Fahad and Crown Prince Abdullah. That cumbersome feudal method was used to assure that all would support the new king. A Saudi's word is supposed to be his bond. That televised procedure was typical of the way the 'head-man' government operates; administrators may have delegated duties but they usually did not delegate decision making power. In each instance, when a decision was required, a person had to approach the head man.

I personally had that experience on many occasions. When I required an administrative decision, I must needs go to the office of the "head-man" such as the dean, the department head, or the director and go into his office, approach his desk, watch him for acknowledgement of my presence, and wait for him to ask my reason for coming. Often, others would come in the middle of my transaction and distract his attention away from me and my problem. But eventually, there would be a disposition of what was at hand. And while such a method may be neither more or less efficient nor time consuming that waiting for out "chain of command", it does require a certain attitude of equality with the headman, an idea well supported in Islam, that each individual is equal in the eyes of God. The fact that I was a woman usually did not cause the "head-man" to take up my matter first as it invariably did in the post office.

Wilfred Thesiger (1981) the intrepid British traveler of the forties, made the following comment upon the Arabs approach to government:

> "Arabs rule but do not administer. Their government is intensely individualistic, and is successful or unsuccessful according to the degree of fear and respect which the ruler commands, and his skill in dealing with individual men. Founded on an individual life, their government is impermanent and liable to end in chaos at any moment."

My feelings exactly! I was aware of that impermanence constantly during my residence there. Turkish people do not like being called Arabs. Though they are Muslims for the most part, they are Turkic people. None-the-less,

Turkey is neighbor. There was a Turkish Coup during the years I was there, as well as the Iran-Iraq War, Sadat's assassination in Egypt, the continuation of the Lebanese Civil War and the Israeli invasion of Lebanon. All these things happening around us reinforced the feeling that the Saudis were precariously perched in their monarchy.

After the Mecca Grand Mosque takeover in 1979, the royal family became very repressive as a self-protective device. Apparently they feared that any assemblage might turn into a plot against them because they issued edicts to the effect that large groups could not meet. In my journal for February 1981, I wrote:

> "On the bus on the way to visit Abdul-Aziz's Murraba Palace, Jennifer was passing back membership money to the women who had been members of the Riyadh International Women's Club, which had held monthly meetings. The last one was in the Riyadh Palace Hotel and had over 1000 in attendance. There is a law here since Mecca that not more than 10 unrelated people shall meet together even in somebody's home. I wonder if this means also women at weddings. So this group that is very culturally positive toward the Saudis is disbanded. And they are compelled to return membership funds. However, I heard last night that they will continue to meet informally in women's villas."

Another group to which I belonged was a natural history organization which had been meeting unofficially for five years to share knowledge about the desert. The specter of being closed down always haunted us. Firstly, it was difficult to find a place to meet, ever since the Mecca takeover. But by the grace of an enlightened dean, we were able to meet in one of the University teaching theatres. But at the end of both my academic years, we were told we would not be allowed to meet there in the fall. The members then explored the possibility of using a hotel auditorium. The hotel was willing but warned us that within a few months of our beginning meetings there, we could be investigated, which would possibly end with our being forbidden to meet, in the same way the International Women's Club had ended. And we had the even more offensive problem of allowing men and women to sit together in the same room to listen to the lectures.

Part of the goal and function of that group was to help people safely enjoy the desert. To fulfill this aim, we sponsored and led outings into the desert. These were well attended so that it was necessary to exercise caution about assembling along known routes. It necessitated our breaking into smaller groups of vehicles rather than one big caravan. We would specify a meeting place just off a main road. When more than ten cars assembled, we would send them off down the road to another point to wait so that no big groups of cars could be seen from the main road. On one occasion, we were a little tardy in sending off the first ten cars. Sure enough, a well dressed Saudi man pulled to the head of the line and began asking questions. I referred him to our leader who spoke good Arabic and then I ran back to the front car and off we went.

Their paranoia following the Mecca takeover was sometimes carried to laughable extremes. In my December 1980 journal entry, more than one year after the takeover, I wrote:

> "An interesting tidbit I learned today is that chess sets were banned from importation last year because the purpose of the game is to KILL THE KING. Here, they couldn't even allow a game with such a purpose after the Mecca Grand Mosque occupation."

At the time of that writing, I wasn't even sure what they said on the box because I had never specifically looked for chess sets. But upon my beginning to work with paraplegic patients, one of the games they asked me for was CHESS. So in my attempt to involve them in activities that interested them, I began to look for chess sets. Sure enough, there was not a whole set to be found. I did find one in a toy store which apparently was a "pre-Mecca-takeover" item as it was in a soiled battered box and was missing several pieces. The final outcome was that I got the patients to make their own chessboard of cardboard. For the chessmen and women, I got the patient to use felt pens and color some of the little plastic "communion glasses" I had scavenged after the communion service from one of the Christian observances. Occupational therapists are famous scavengers! It just tickles me to think of an Islamic king and queen made out of Christian communion cups.

Later, the Saudi social worker saw this "jimmied up" occupational therapy project in use and told the patients that he would go out and buy one for the treatment unit. It was not fitting that those Saudi patients should use such a crude looking set. He forgot, of course, that less than thirty years ago, almost every item used by his people was crude and handmade. Also, he undermined the goal of my therapy which was to induce patients to become involved with the manufacture of "useful" items. But to my great glee, he, too was unsuccessful at finding a chess set. Unfortunately, the stigma he had cast on the homemade set caused it to be used no further. So no further KILL THE KING tournaments occurred.

In chapter nine, I referred to being stopped by the police when I was riding with a man. We were lucky that time because those village police even exceeded the city police in the level of their "police state" paranoia. Our two vehicles were headed south out to some unexplored *jebels* or mountains. In the front Land Rover was a family of four. In the next four-wheel drive was the driver and myself. We both knew it was deemed "illegal privacy" for us to be riding together in the front seat since we were both single, but we had done it often enough to have lost our fear of being caught. However on this occasion, our route led directly through the village and past the police station. They came out and stopped us. The couple in front were old-timers at this and talked so sweetly, that the policeman motioned us through, not bothering to check our papers. When we got just beyond the village, the driver of my car realized he had left his gas cap back at the gas station before the village. I decided I was not going to brave that police station again with a man to whom I was not married. So I got into the vehicle with the family while my companion headed back. We drove ahead and found a pleasant little hill by which to wait for him. We'd been there but a few minutes when a Toyota truck with two men approached. One got out and came over to talk to us, two innocent looking women, two children and a man. He informed us that he was the police and "What are you doing here?" He had followed us. We told him we just wanted to camp in their lovely *wadi* which was a plausible enough answer since many city Arabs took to the desert on cool weekends. He attempted more conversation. But up came a car with two more men in it. They called to the policeman talking to us and told him to come along. They all drove off and we breathed a sigh of relief, only to realize a few minutes later that they were on top of another hill across the *wadi* watching us with field-glasses. Meanwhile my driver had been detained at the police station until he agreed to sit down and drink tea with them. We were beginning to be a little anxious about his prolonged absence when we sighted him coming down the *wadi*. It was with great pleasure that we drove away from that village. This sort of "Western custom vs. Saudi law" situation was the cause of most of my anxiety during my two years. Things that seemed natural in the USA were against laws and traditions in Saudi Arabia. One horror story that kept me anxious and on my toes for months after I heard it, was of the American nurse who went on a week long camping trip with two men. Some provincial police came upon their camp, discovered they were all unrelated, so tied up her two companions and raped her. She could do nothing legally since she had broken the law first. She was at their mercy or lack of it.

Like all governments, some of the regulations created hilarious SNAFU

(Situation Normal All Fucked Up) circumstances. In my journal I have one told to me by a friend who was the "warden" of his American government compound. This job involved attending monthly "warden" meetings and passing on the information to the other residents in his compound. The US government organized this system to protect people in the months following the Iran hostage events

I wrote:

> "At the meeting they told them 'Absolutely <u>never</u> stop to help anybody who has had a car accident or any other kind of accident.'. Apparently, if you were in any way involved, they blame you, the Westerner for the accident and arrest you, too. For example, a Lebanese man employed by the US government, had a heart attack. His brother was present. The brother is a doctor and tried to revive him but was unsuccessful. So the brother is in jail. Then it took the US government about a week to get the body shipped out. They wouldn't let them put it in the local morgue where it could be in cold storage. And since he was dead he couldn't sign his exit visa, so they gave our government officials all kinds of trouble about it until the body was really ripe."

One of the areas in which I predict the Saudis will have future trouble is their continued attempt to enforce traditional puritanical Wahabi ideals in conduct and in government while at the same time attempting to acquire and maintain the latest in technology. An example of this is their fasting law, which non-fasters may not eat, drink or smoke in front of fasters without risking arrest. Yet they have been presented the medical facts regarding the dangers of fasting from water during the extremes of desert heat. Intellectually they know that what they are doing is dangerous, yet they cannot reinterpret the Prophet's instructions in line with modern health practices, modern technology of medicine.

W. Montgomery Watt (1961) had this to say on the subject:

> "In the case of social changes, ideation and activity are normally parallel in a mature society, in that before a course of action is adopted, it has to be seen to be in accordance with (that is, integrated into) the tradition of the society, both of ideation and of action. A mature society hesitates about a novel course of action until it finds a satisfactory link between the action and ideational tradition."

The Saudis have accepted most modern technology and especially medicine while yet retaining the attitude that all health is *En Sha Allah* or "if God wills it". Additionally there is no way to fast from water in extreme heat and feel good, but since it was prescribed by the Prophet, it supersedes modern knowledge of body fluid balance.

Unless they do become more able to integrate technology into their religious structure, I predict that they will be unable to have or handle the world leadership for which they strive. Part of the problem was the newness of their association with science and technology. Part of it stems from their continuing presentation of the image that their labor and crafts are low status employments with administration and commerce being the only respectable professions.

REFERENCES:

Ali, Abdallah Yousef (1931) *The Quran*, Egypt.

Thesiger, Wilfred (1981) *Arabian Sands*. New York: Penguin Books.

Watt, W. Montgomery (1961). *Islam and the Integration of Society*. London: Routledge & Kegan Paul, Ltd.

12

JUSTICE

While the Koran may have said little about government, it said a great deal about justice, and indeed justice was the topic that dominated Saudi culture. Since the law of the country was based on the *shari'ah* they interpreted it very literally. I did my best to stay clear of involvement with their justice system, feeling sure that my American interpretation of an English language version of the Koran (Ali, 1931) would greatly differ from their Saudi interpretation of the original written Arabic, Recently, a new translation into Urdu, published in Pakistan, was forbidden for importation into Saudi Arabia where there are many thousands of Pakistani workers because Saudi religious teachers disagreed with some new interpretations they felt the translator has made. Urdu uses the same alphabet with many common words. So I felt sure my English translation and ideas would not concur with the meaning accepted by judges in an Islamic court.

> ### Sura IV Verse 135
> *Ye who believe!*
> *Stand out firmly*
> *For justice, as witnesses*
> *To God, even as against*
> *Yourselves, or your parents,*
> *Or your kin, and whether*
> *It be (against) rich or poor;*
> *For God can best protect both..*

Follow not the lusts
(of your hearts), lest ye
Swerve, and if ye
Distort (justice) or decline
To do justice, verily
God is well-acquainted
With all that ye do.

Anything I heard about dealings in the Islamic courts were that the judges were fair to the extreme, within their laws, but once a verdict was announced then the harshness began. Or we Westerners interpret it as harshness. But as you can see from the previous Sura, they were admonished to administer justice.

Sura V Verse 41
As to the thief
Male or female,
Cut off his or her hands:
A punishment by way
Of example, from God,
For their crime:
And God is exalted in Power.

When I originally decided to take the job in Saudi Arabia I joked with my co-professionals that I was being imported to teach thieves with only one hand to learn to work or to be trained in one handed tasks which was a big part of traditional occupational therapy. During my stay, I saw only one one-handed beggar and that was during the last week in Riyadh. I read only one report of judiciary amputation while there. It was not done frequently or rashly. In my journal I had this to say about the topic;

> "And all that stuff about 'no thievery in Saudi is not true. Several people in the American/British community have reported stolen briefcases out of locked cars and even stolen cars. In the book on ibn Saud, *The Desert King* by David Howarth (1964) tells how when Americans first came here 35 years before, they would turn in thieves until they learned that the thieves, often their own servants, had their hands cut off, so they stopped turning them in. So the Saudis learned 'You can steal from Americans.'"

The most well publicized act of Saudi justice was the beheading of the two Filipino rape/murderers in Riyadh January 29, 1982. This obviously upset many Americans because three of my friends wrote letters of their horror upon hearing of the event and two others sent clippings from American newspapers. I became aware of the event while at a dinner party in a friend's apartment. I was alone there with three married men friends when we four sat drinking after dinner coffee and waiting for the fifteen minutes of English news on TV. Suddenly, the announcer changed tack and announced that the two men who had been beheaded that day in "Chop Square, the name Westerners had for the execution place, had re-enacted the crime for police before the execution and a film of this re-enactment would be shown. They then did indeed, show these two docile Filipino servants speaking in English and explaining to the police each step of their crimes. In one scene, one of the plainclothesmen officers who was dressed in *thobe* and *ghutra*, did appear to be coaching, but otherwise, it all seemed very voluntary. In my journal I wrote this:

> "They had Saudi men playing the parts of the victims who were a Lebanese couple. First, they showed them hitting the wife in the side of the neck, carrying her out, raping her and then waiting for the husband to come home, killing him with a steel pipe, then taking the jewelry, ripping open the small home safe. The two accused men told their story in English since it is the second language here and most Filipinos speak it. They even had them go through part of the story twice, once in English, once in Tagalog, the national language of the Philippines. Then after the English news, they replayed it three more times, once in Tagalog all the way through and then in Arabic twice. The Arabic speaking dinner guest said it was just a translation of the English used by the criminals and the police during the filming."

They played the tape again the following day in Arabic and Tagalog. I was really concerned for the Filipino community since I had become friendly with several women. I felt sure this television showing would have repercussions on them and it did. When I went into the hospital to work a day later, it had already started. Filipina nurses who were supposed to have left for holiday, had been detained, their passports sent through for police check and their luggage searched. A woman who accompanied several Filipina rape victims to court as translator remarked to me "You can just imagine what is happening to private servants inside these walled villas as a result of that 'anti-Filipino' TV show."

Another friend whose daughter attended the same school as the daughter of the victims, reported the girl saying these two servants 'were always on drugs." I felt they must have been drugged during the performance of the TV re-enactment. They seemed absolutely without emotion as they went through their crime. No sorrow, no revulsion, and no fear!

In the English newspapers, there was no advance notice of when the beheading would take place, but an acquaintance of mine had chosen that day to try to fulfill a promise to himself to attend an execution. When he had been home in summer, many people said to him, "Did you see a beheading?" Because of this, he felt obliged to satisfy their curiosity. Hence his presence on that day. He described it to me thus; "These two Filipinos looked so ordinary, except they had the back of their heads and necks shaved up to the crown. They were wearing T-shirts and blue jeans, had ankle chains, hands and elbows manacled behind them. They had on red blindfolds as they walked out, knelt down before the executioner who said some verses of the Koran. There was an aggressive young policeman in front pushing the crowd back. At the moment of the execution, the policeman fainted."

When I discussed my feelings that the two had been drugged during the TV filming, this acquaintance said, "Ah, yes, of course, that is why they were so docile during the pre-execution moments. They acted drugged." The media never said drugs were given to any convicted person before execution. But I felt sure that drugs were administered. Gradually, the Saudis were using more 'humane' methods, judged from a Westerners point of view. For example, they no longer just lopped off the hand in the square. It was done as a proper aseptic surgical procedure. So I think it is fair to assume that they would also allow prisoners the solace of drugs before execution. Most surely, those men were promised pre-execution drugs as a form of bribe for their cooperation with the TV filming. These may seem small steps to Westerners who still argue about the ethics of capital punishment, but in a culture where justice had traditionally always been swift and harsh, it was a 'humane' change.

In the same arbitrary way most justice systems operate, they were not consistent. They often appeared to make examples of people or groups.

Sura IV Verse 15
If any of your women
Are guilty of lewdness,
Take the evidence of four
(Reliable) witnesses from amongst you
Against them; and if they testify,
Confine them to houses until

114

Death do claim them,
Or God ordain for them
Some (other) way.

Verse 16
If two men among you
Are guilty of lewdness,
Punish them both.
If they repent and amend,
Leave them alone; for God
Is Oft-returning, Most Merciful.

One of my friends worked at the King's specialist hospital and reported that there had been a sudden increase of surveillance on single women. She went on to say that her Saudi colleagues said they expected someone to be made an example of soon. She told me this as a warning, because though I did not work there, she was aware that I was in a drama group. She said I should be especially careful as they were beginning to pick up people attending music and drama groups. Entertainments such as these had historically been forbidden and were only tolerated now as long as they were fairly invisible. But upon occasion, the mutawahs would exert themselves for greater purity and begin to ferret out "entertainments" and close them.

Sura XXIV Verse 2
The woman of man
Guilty of adultery or fornication
Flog each of them
With a hundred stripes:
Let not compassion move you
In their case, in a matter
Prescribed by God, if ye believe
In God and the Last Day:
And let a party
Of the Believers
Witness their punishment.

Verse 3
Let no man guilty of
Adultery or fornication marry
Any but a woman

Similarly guilty, or an Unbeliever:

Verse 4
And those who launch
A charge against chaste women,
And produce not four witnesses
(To support their allegations), --
Flog them with eighty stripes;
And reject their evidence
Ever after: for such men
Are wicked transgressors; --

The dealer of justice is admonished to flog fornicators and adulterers without compassion, however, the punishment for women that I heard about most commonly was stoning. Friends, who lived in Riyadh seven years, recounted the stonings they saw when they lived on the second floor of a block of flats on a main street. The noise of the approaching crowd would draw them to the window. The condemned woman would usually be trying to outrun the crowd, tripping over her long skirts. On more than one occasion, the woman was rescued when a vehicle drew abreast of her and pulled her in, thus saving her life.

After having someone tell me of the presentation of a 'doctored' marriage certificate to her employer in order to be allowed to have her lover live with her, I wrote the following thoughts in my journal:

> "Since adultery is a severely punished crime here, she had to find a way to make it appear legal. If they were to be found out, probably all they would do is send her home, but the law does prescribe STONING for women. They bury her up to her neck in sand and then just stone her to death."

Though I heard of this punishment being meted out by the court, I could find no reference to it in the Koran. Lashes were the only punishment for sexual misbehavior.

Most British and Americans are more familiar with the account of the shooting execution as punishment in the film "Death of a Princess". I had not wanted to watch it when it was presented for viewing a few months before my departure for Riyadh. Fortunately, one of my friends was lucky enough to get a copy of this forbidden video in Saudi Arabia. When the BBC first showed it, Saudi Arabia cut off relations with Britain. Though I never heard any information which indicated the degree of veracity of the film, I can verify that the crowd scenes, in the way in which people bunched, talked to and looked at each other were very authentic. It seemed impossible that it could have been filmed in any place but Riyadh. However, I learned later it was filmed in Egypt. I realized how easily I was duped.

The city police were different from the mutawahs. The most obvious difference was that the mutawahs were old men with red henna dyed beards and wore *thobes*, while the civil police were young and wore kaki uniforms and carried guns The mutawahs carried only their staves. And engineer I knew was called to the police barracks to assess an electrical malfunction. I wrote his description and my reaction to it:

> "Two large cement barracks of about 40 yards by 40 yards with no furniture. The police live there, living out of suitcases, sleeping on a blanket on the cement floor. Seventy men to one large cubicle like that. The toilet is a hole in the floor, the same as it is everywhere here except in my apartment and two of them serve seventy men. There are no bathing facilities, just a water tap on some white tile, now black with dirt, with the spigot about one foot off the floor. So it is impossible for them to get their body under it, just their feet and hands and then to splash some on their faces. With this hot temperature and the seventy of them in the same room, it must get quite fragrant sometimes in summer.
>
> And also, since washing hands, face, mouth, ears and feet before every one of their five daily prayer times must really put a strain on their facilities.
>
> He also said the kitchen was an abomination. Perhaps he exaggerated, but he said the walls had an inch of food stuck to them, like they had never been cleaned. I guess these folks come from just off the desert with mud villages where the wind just blows dirt away, so they never had to worry about it before.
>
> But my thought on this was that these fellows, who live in such primitive conditions, wouldn't think living in their jails is such horrible punishment because it wouldn't be much different from what they live in at home. Therefore, they have little compunction about consigning anyone there.
>
> People are arrested here for many slight things. The jails provide minimal food, no pure water. An inmate's friends or family must find out where they are being kept as there are

many different jails in the city and then must bring them the necessities of life or they could just die there."

I later learned that in some men's prisons, the food was served to prisoners from a wheelbarrow. One man I knew of who had minor back trouble before he was jailed came out a cripple because he got a diet without calcium, no sunlight, no exercise and had to sleep on the cold cement floor and yes it is cold on the floor even in Saudi Arabia. He was found "not guilty".

One time, I did accompany a friend who made regular visits to the women's prison. I found that the women were better provided for than the men I heard from. When we approached the prison, the only indication that it was different from any of the surrounding villas, was the uniformed policeman sitting near a wooden guard shack the size of a telephone booth on the sidewalk. Otherwise it looked just like the other walls on the street. There was no barbed wire on top. As we walked up to the gate, the parcels and bags we brought were examined by the guard. He pointed for us to set them on the sidewalk. Then we entered into the courtyard which was about twelve yards by six yards in size. A female got up from a crude wooden bench against the wall of a small house and came forward to frisk us. It was a thorough job, feeling between legs from foot to crotch under our long dresses, squeezing our breasts to make sure no hard objects were carried there. It became obvious that the guard knew my friend and knew she hated to be frisked. Also, perhaps she liked her blond hair and fair skin, as she squeezed my friend's breasts twice, much to her anger and dismay. But a Saudi prison is no place to create a fuss. Then we turned to the side of the courtyard where the visitors could see the inmates. My friend had women she regularly came to see, all of whom spoke English since my friend spoke no other language. She assigned me to talk to two Sri Lankan women who were accused of stealing from the woman they worked for. The inmate and her sister claimed that the husband had attempted sexual involvement with them which the wife discovered, thus accusing them of thievery to get them out of the house. My friend went to talk to two Filipino women who were both incarcerated for sex outside of marriage. It was a real task to get close enough to the three layer mesh fence to see the women. The wire meshes were of three different sizes so they effectively cut off any clear view of the people I was talking to. The side of the fence where the prisoners were was a cement courtyard of nearly double the size of ours. The prisoners were all crowded up against their side of the fifteen foot high mesh. On our side, the first comers sat cross-legged on the carpets as close to the fence as possible as they talked to the women they came to visit. Latecomers had to stand behind those sitters and squatters. I was in the third row back from the fence. It was really difficult to talk to people whose second language was English from a distance of about two yards with three layers of mesh wire between. Arabs have no compunction about jostling and using elbows to assist them to advance to their destination. So much of my visit was a 'holding pattern'. During this sequence, our bags and parcels for the inmates had been brought in by the female guards and placed on a table by the wall in the visitors' courtyard. My friend gave the one English speaking guard some instructions about the package. The women I was visiting asked for some warm socks. Then it was time to go. When we got back into the car where her husband was waiting to drive us home, my friend unrolled several tiny scrolls of paper which the prisoners had pushed through the mesh and asked her to deliver to various friends or to mail back home to their countries. I was amazed at how she had gotten close enough to the fence to accomplish that. She'd been visiting for nearly a year and had become practiced at this since it was the only way they could get word out to family and friends about their situations. One of the Filipina women was to go to court the following Saturday and was anxious for word to be gotten to her lover in the men's prison to tell the same story she told and to never confess, lest they be given their 100 lashes. On the way home my friend puzzled about what man she knew who would go to the men's prison at the visiting hours and push the Tagalog note through the mesh to him before time for the court appearance. It was so exciting though I never went back. Bad for the blood pressure! Their whole justice system was bad for my blood pressure!

REFERENCES:

Ali, Abdallah Yousef (1931) *The Quran*, Egypt.

13

ART, MUSIC & RECREATION

Sura VII Verse 137
And We made a people
Considered weak (And of no account),
Inheritors of lands
In both East and West,--
Lands whereon We sent
Down Our Blessings
The fair promise of the Lord
Was fulfilled for the Children
Of Israel, because they had
Patience and constancy,
And We leveled to the ground
The great Works and fine Buildings
Where Pharaoh and his people
Erected (with such pride).

Verse 138
We took the Children of Israel
(With safety) across the sea.
They came upon a people
Devoted entirely to some idols
They had. They said:

"O Moses! Fashion for us
A god like unto the gods
They have." He said:
"Surely ye are a people
Without knowledge.

Verse 139
"As to these folk,--
The cult they are in
Is (but) a fragment of a ruin,
And vain is the (worship)
Which they practice."

It was interesting and a little bewildering that the Saudis wanted me, an art therapist and also an occupational therapist to teach in a country where prohibitions against art were evident throughout the city. Sign boards with human figures on them frequently had the faces obliterated with spray paint. Even graffiti pictures with faces had them effaced. Clothing displays hung in windows with no manikins.

Art therapy is a kind of therapy that attempts to get a person to visualize their problems instead of acting them out. And sometimes they are encouraged to use visual imagery to see solutions to their problems. As you can imagine, this form of treatment would not be popular in a country where the very human forms have been kept from view. To produce them, to expose them on paper, canvas or in clay or photography was going against deep cultural/ religious attitudes. The various kinds of Arabic language calligraphy have been the main form of art in Saudi Arabia and may, in addition to architecture continue to be, in the future. There seemed to be a little loosening of restrictions on art, but basically, the human form was still forbidden. It was OK to draw and photograph buildings, but not people, and especially not women.

Truck decoration was described in Chapter Nine on Transportation but it deserves to be acknowledged in the field of art, too, since it is one of the few indigenous expressions of art that I saw. Decorating modes of transportation is a world wide phenomenon. Camels, donkeys, and horses have worn gorgeous tassels, woven strips and embellished leather harnesses on special occasions, as well as on a daily basis in most countries I have visited ; Mexico, Turkey, Greece, and Egypt. An especially lovely travel accoutrement in the Middle East was the camel bag, woven of bright colored wool in traditional tribal patterns. They were great sellers in the antique souq in Riyadh.

Jewelry, as an art form, flourished for women but not for men. Men were cautioned against wearing jewelry in public, except wristwatches. And since women were covered up in public nobody knew what they wore underneath, except that almost every Saudi woman had a wrist full of gold bangles. Some said it was traditionally a woman's retirement insurance, though it was no longer necessary under their social security insurance system. But when those women took off their veils and *abayas*, they had some of the most fantastic jewelry I've ever seen worn on a daily basis. The students wore gold and platinum pendants encrusted with emeralds, rubies, diamonds and pearls to class. The cleaning women wore so many bangles, dangling earrings and necklaces, I wondered how they were able to keep from catching on everything such as faucets, hinges, knobs, and railings, but they managed gracefully.

Lots of jewelry worn all the time by women, was historically commonplace, in that peninsula. Since jewelry was money, it included many coins worked into the designs. The Bedouin silver jewelry in which the ratio of silver to copper varied greatly, which was seen in the several souqs, and had coinage from throughout the world. It was soldered and wired together. I seldom saw it worn except by 'artistic' Westerners. It could still be purchased at reasonable prices for such lovely hand-crafted work; so many Westerners undertook the hobby of collecting it, since "souqing" was a permissible entertainment.

> "Great nations write their autobiography in three manuscripts: the book of their words, the book of their deeds and the book of their art. Not one of these books can be understood unless we read the other two, but of the three, the only one quite trustworthy is the last."
>
> *John Ruskin*

This comment, when applied to Saudi Arabia as a method of analysis in predicting whether it will endure to 'greatness' might reveal the following;

The list of books of their words would be headed by the *Koran*, since all language of literature is judged by its purity in relation to that classical Arabic. It is as if we continue to judge the literary worth of our literature on whether the language was still as pure as *Beowulf*, since *Beowulf* was written about 1 thirteen hundred years ago and the *Koran* was written about fourteen hundred years ago. They do not want or expect their language to evolve since it is 'the word of God'. Just think what it would be like if we all judged every letter, every article and every book on whether it read like Beowulf?

Most of the books of their deeds have been written within the last century, since hardly anybody at all wrote anything before that. Literacy was and still is a problem. During my visits to the 'old city' in Riyadh, I could always see a scribe or two writing letters for customers while seated on a carpet in a shaded alley. Because there is so little recorded history, that peninsula is an archeologist's paradise, if an archeologist could get a visa, and if she or he could get permission to dig. Most archeological sites are open and unprotected. Even the famous Al-Fau, of which a British movie was made, was visited by friends in 1982. The guard was absent so they drove right into the ancient site.

The books of Saudi Arabian art are few and far between. Most books by Western painters were approved by the Ministry of Information during the last decade. The prohibition against 'graven images' is still so strong, that two artists I met recounted having had their sketch pads grabbed from their hands and destroyed before their eyes. One friend who was giving an exhibition of her work at one of the few art galleries, was obliged to submit all her pictures several weeks ahead so that the religious censor could judge them to see if any should not be allowed.

I felt sure that the Prophet, being a wise man, had not intended these extreme restrictions on normal human expression. I felt vindicated when, on my return trip through Egypt, I found the following commentary on "Islam's attitude toward the representation of living creatures" by Egypt's Ministry of Culture U. A. R. (1969);

> "The widespread opinion has often held that figural representation was prohibited by the *Qur'an* but in fact, this subject is not mentioned in any of the verses of the *Qur'an*. Where the second Islamic legislative source – The Traditions of the Prophet – was concerned, portraiture seems to have been disapproved of but not altogether proscribed. Portraits could be displayed only in places where they could not be mistaken as objects of reverence. It is still the prevailing opinion that this aversion to portraiture was meant to prevent the early Muslims from the use of human and animal motifs both in pictorial decoration and in sculpture, though earlier theologians on occasion condemned their appearance in places and private homes, doubtless because they disapproved of excessive Royal luxury."

As an art therapist, I have pondered many times about the success the religious teachers had in rooting out the natural instinct to draw or to visualize people near and dear to us. I was able to be present during a session in which the psychiatrist asked a girl she was evaluating for possible mental retardation to draw a man, the best man she could possibly draw. The child did draw a picture congruent with her ten year old abilities. The man wore a thobe, ghutra and igal. She completed it by making a sharp slashing line across his neck. The doctor asked her why? The child explained that that effectually invalidated the picture as an idol. Already she had an ingrained idea about the prohibition against representing human figures in her art. I wondered if the ancient Arabs of centuries ago had so much sand in their eyes, they could not see so they disguised their inability by forbidding art. But David Howarth (1964) had a better explanation:

> " . . . Arabs are bad at describing each other . . . It is obvious, from the former architecture, etc. that they were not a visual people, which gives rise to all kinds of conjectures about why. For one thing, since the Wahabis forbade images, they would be unlikely to scrutinize as the artist does. Also, when everyone, more or less dressed alike, they would be difficult to distinguish. And since the Koran was the only literature, it is my belief that the language could not have blossomed with many descriptive phrases."

In Jeddah, which had been an international seaport for centuries, the big outdoor sculptures had been placed in prominent spots around the city. I never saw them except in someone else's slides. Apparently, Riyadh was attempting to replicate this form of art expression. Before I ever arrived, there was a display of enormous Saudi coffee pots, the national symbol of hospitality, on a raised circular plot of grass in the center of the airport traffic circle. During my second year, another sculpture in the form of a human hand appeared over the corner near my bus stop. In a hand, which must have been six yards high, were clutched some pipes or wires. A Saudi friend explained that as this symbol was over the Islamic Center for Youth, it represented youth's work and recreation.

In a country where public entertainments were forbidden, many people developed new hobbies to fill time. Photography blossomed despite the need for rigorous observance of their 'image' prohibitions. Some expatriate camera bugs claimed the cameras were cheaper than the ones in their home countries. When I compared the cheap type with which I am familiar, the Saudi cameras imported from Japan, Italy and Germany were just as expensive as cameras 'on sale' in American catalogues. During my initial job interview, I had asked whether I could bring my camera. The response was yes, but make sure you take a Saudi Muslim out with you when you go shooting so they can tell you what is permissible to photograph. I decided that seemed too cumbersome so did not take my camera the first year. But after watching all the others, I decided to bring mine with me the second year when I returned after my holiday at home in California. I was then able to photograph in many situations where my male acquaintances could never have been present. Then I could show them the pictures of the half of life that they were missing by not being able to see women and what they did. However, it was not permitted to just go around photographing women. Before a Saudi woman could be photographed, it was necessary to ask her permission. Some of the more conservative ones refused on the basis that their male relatives were the only ones who would ever be permitted to see their faces. Another reason given to me by a student was when she asked me to never show her picture to a Western male, because men just got so sexually excited looking at pictures of women that it was sinful to tempt them. When during my last few weeks I decided I wanted some photographs of the campus and the masses of female students, I found it was necessary to be extremely careful. I barred the unlockable bathroom door with a rubbish can and stood on the toilet seat to take my photograph through the six inch slit in the restroom window. I then climbed four stories to the unfenced roof of the English Building and took photographs straight down hoping the students would not look up and catch me for then I would be in trouble.

On several occasions, I saw women I was with scolded for using their cameras in the wrong place. While on the train to Dammam, my friend was told to stop taking pictures of those miles of sand. Ostensibly there must have been some military structures she might be spying out. On another occasion, an American consultant insisted on bringing her camera on a trip to the souq, despite our warnings against it. She was just ready to click the shutter when a mutawah came running up waving his arms to prevent her photographing two willing veiled teenagers. So she put her camera away. I felt she was lucky to have escaped that easily since several men I knew reported having film ripped from their cameras. In fact, one was taking his camera to be repaired when the mutawah thrust open the empty camera in an attempt to destroy the film. As soon as the mutawah who had cautioned my American consultant disappeared, the two teenagers through sign language persuaded her to take their pictures surreptitiously in a nearby alley. But they kept their veils down.

Another friend brought back a beautiful clay bust of Nefertiti from a group tour of Egypt. As she went through Saudi customs, she worried but the agent did not ask her to open her suitcase. However, the man in line behind her had a suitcase full of antique weapons; swords, daggers; needless to say, importing weapons from Egypt into Saudi Arabia is forbidden. They confiscated all of them and began going through the luggage of the remainder of the group. All the others who had brought back similar clay busts, watched with horrified eyes as the customs man smashed them.

In a letter to one of my musician friends at home I described my experience with music:

"Only 100 years ago, they were still putting people in prison for even possessing a musical instrument in this city. A few days ago, as I got ready to walk home from the University School of Nursing when it was in the villa, I started singing to the gatekeeper's wife and two Egyptian office workers. Well, as we walked out of the 14 foot high gate to the street, we said goodbye to the gatekeeper who was sitting down on the rug in front of his little house near the gate with an open Koran in front of him. He usually smiles and says "Ma Salama!" or "Be Safe"! But he apparently didn't like us to be singing to his wife because he completely ignored us. His wife loved the singing.

"I have met a man here who collects old Middle Eastern musical instruments. He has a thing like a violin but with thirty five wire strings and three that are out of some thing like waxed hemp. On Thursdays, sometimes we go to the music souq where they sell old instruments.

There is a current Saudi instrument called 'the *rababa*' which has one string and is played with a crude bow. It is tuned by heating it over the fire. It is an accompanying instrument for the singing voice in the Middle East. One night at a dinner party, there was a man who claimed to have been born in a Bedouin tent in Iraq who sang a few songs of his youth for us. He obviously had a strong voice and felt comfortable performing. But his songs were so strange, alien, lonely and sad though he said they were "love songs".

I shipped my autoharp over. It is the only thing I play and usually only for myself, to accompany myself on American 'folk songs'. But since I've been here, since there us such a paucity of music and musicians, I have played publicly. One day, I took my autoharp to work and played for the psychiatric nursing students. And within a few minutes, every teacher and students had heard the music and come to the classroom. Live music is such an unusual occurrence here."

Except at ladies parties! There we would dance with abandon to both traditional Saudi and Egyptian music as well as American and English rock. At one of our department parties our secretary began dancing, then some of the little daughters of the staff joined. The secretary tied scarves around their hips so the hip movement which predominates in Egyptian dancing would show more. Then our Bedouin tea lady, who had her heavy hair below her waist loosened for the first time since I met her, danced. The Saudi dances involve a bouncing kind of step while using the head and neck like a flagpole to wave the long banner of hair. Some dances involved coyly moving past a female partner while peeping around the hands.

Carom was a popular game. It was played in the same way we play it, on a board with mesh pockets. And they substitute button or checkers for missing caroms in the same way I played it in my youth. Another game which men reported often playing at outdoor meals called 'goat grabs' was *Beloti*, in which a grid of holes was made in the sand; then small pebbles were tossed in various holes. The women never played either game in my presence. Cards were not popular because of the Koranic prohibition against gambling.

Soccer absorbed a lot of attention and emotional energy from the Western men I knew. Sports news of which soccer was the biggest news maker, took up the last two or three minutes of the fifteen minutes of daily English news. It was allotted the same amount of time on the Arabic news. I never tried to attend a game but was told by a male colleague who did that women were not permitted in the stadium with the men.

REFERENCES:

Ali, Abdallah Yousef (1931) *The Quran*, Egypt.

Howarth, David (1964) *The Desert King: The Life of Ibn Saud*. Beirut, Librairie du Liban.

Ross, Heather Colyer (1978) *Bedouin Jewelry in Saudi Arabia*. London: Stacey International.

Ministry of Culture U. A. R. (April, 1969) "Islamic Art in Egypt" 969-1517. Exhibition in the Semiramis Hotel, Cairo, Egypt.

14

RELIGION

Sura III Verse 83
Do they seek
For other than the Religion
Of God? – while all creatures
In the heavens and on earth
Have, willingly or unwillingly,
Bowed to His Will
(Accepted Islam)
And to Him shall they
All be brought back.

The state religion which is the only legal one in Saudi Arabia was started by the Prophet Mohammad who was born in Mecca in 570 AD. He started his religious career preaching there. His fellow townsmen didn't take kindly to his message about the 'True God'. He fled to Medina to the north and from there, began the spread of Islam. The city of his birth did come to accept his new faith eventually. However, he continued to live and finally to die in Medina. Because both of these 'holy' cities are in Saudi Arabia, it gives that country a special place in the Islamic world community

The Prophet apparently was not literate enough to write down what he said, so some of his followers wrote it down after his death. Moslems claim that the *Koran* is the spoken voice of Allah as revealed to Mohammad. Many of his teaching are from the 'traditions' which were made into the book *The Hadith*. *The Hadith* contains forty separate lessons. They are much easier reading than the *Koran*.

Islam has five 'pillars' upon which it rests. Firstly, the believer must testify that there is no god save Allah and that Mohammad is his messenger. Secondly, he or she must perform the five daily prayers; daybreak, noon, mid-afternoon, early evening and night. Thirdly, he Muslim must pay the *zakat*, the poor tax or alms. Fourthly, the believer must fast during the month of Ramadan. And lastly, he or she must make the pilgrimage to the Holy Mosque in Mecca. Such simplicity was obviously formulated to fit with the fiercest of desert life. The observance of these rituals, which distracts him or her from the extremes of desert living assured the Muslim entrance into heaven and prevented any guilt or remorse about the past or worry about the future. Apparently the Prophet took bits from the two main monotheistic religions in that region, Judaism and Christianity and added a bit of tribal faith and fashioned a custom-made religion for desert Arabs.

Sura II Verse 130
And who turns away
From the religion of Abraham
But such as debase their souls
With folly? Him we chose
And rendered pure in this world:
And he will be in the Hereafter
In the ranks of the Righteous.

But in the little paperback book given to me by my favorite antique dealer, which is titled *Islam: the Religion of Truth*, the message is strong and clear that I shall not go "Scot free' for saying that Mohammad created the *Koran* when it is the 'revealed' word of God. I am therefore taking my future afterlife in my hands by attempting to tell of its roots.

The daily prayers were a strenuous observance for the faithful, but they also became something of a burden for every other person in Saudi Arabia. All stores closed for every prayer time. The faithful must find some water for ablution and wash feet, hands, eyes, ears, nose and mouth. Every mosque appeared to have its ablution trough. If one were out in the desert where water was unavailable, sand could be used to ceremoniously cleanse.

Sura IV Verse 7
Ye who believe!

Approach not prayers
With a mind befogged.
Until ye can understand
All that ye say, - -
Nor in a state
Of ceremonial impurity
(Except when traveling on he road.)
Until after washing
Your whole body.
If ye are ill,
Or on a journey,
Or one of you cometh
From the offices of nature,
Or ye have been
In contact with women,
And ye find no water,
Then take for yourselves
Clean sand or earth,
And rub therewith
Your faces and hands.
For God doth blot out sins
And forgive again and again.

If there were no mosque available, they would just find any old place to lay down a prayer rug. Women were not allowed in Saudi mosques with men, except the ones in the Holy Places such as Mecca, Medina and the haj route, so they always had to find their own place. Men were encouraged to pray together with the oldest or most learned leading the prayers. I was surprised at how many of my female friends and colleagues did pray faithfully. The bathroom floor in our office and classroom building was always wet after prayer time. It was a common experience for me to walk into a room and find one of them with the prescribed white cotton cloth over her head and shoulders, down on her knees bowing toward Mecca. They seemed oblivious to my entrance. Just how oblivious these worshippers could be I discovered during a shopping trip as I recorded in my journal:

"There is an open market perhaps the size of two city blocks. The shops face out to the surrounding streets and then it is transected by two alleys which are also lined with shops. They are just plywood with tent covers open on one side. Several months ago, one section burned at night with a furious glow

130

that was visible for miles. After they had cleaned part of it up, we were able to see that the burned section was about 120 feet by 200 feet. Not much actually, but apparently part of what was burned was the tent mosque for praying if prayer time came during shopping. The other day as we walked, a prayer call rung out and in the middle of the remaining rubble was a cleared section with some carpets laid down, a loudspeaker on top of a 4 by 4 post and two lines of men bowing toward the west. The one time I truly wished for my camera. It was just so illustrative of how these folks don't appear to notice their surroundings. Prayer is prayer and you just kneel down and do it. No inspiration needed. Of course, this disregard for things carries over into cleanliness and health practices, too."

If the Muslim were devout, it seemed he or she could pray anywhere. While returning from camping, I saw 'lorry drivers' in a sand storm, praying shielded by huge truck tires. Usually, they knelt on one of the cheap garish little prayer rugs which cost approximately $3 in the souq, but sometimes, their knees and foreheads were right on the sand.

Prayer time occurred at approximately 4:30 am, 12:00 noon, 3:30 pm, 6 pm and 8:30 pm. It was different each day depending upon the position of the moon. The moon's rising or setting controlled most of the occurrences in Islam. There was a mosque in every hospital, just as there is a chapel in every hospital in the USA. Since I lived in the University Hospital Staff Residence on the grounds of University Hospital, the mosque was directly beneath my third floor window. I awakened every morning to the sounds of the muezzin or cantor announcing prayers over the loud speaker. He did this each prayer time. I heard his voice for about two minutes. If I stepped out unto the balcony, I saw crowds of men washing their faces and hands and removing their shoes prior to entering the hospital mosque which is a modest one story building with rolls of red and gold carpets placed in rows so worshippers can kneel in a row facing west. 'Prayer time' lasted about one half hour. Then there was another minute of loudspeaker prayer. The worshippers all filed out and unerringly found their own pair of sandals among the mass.

Religious requirements were much less strenuous on women. I heard rumors that Islamic women did not go to Heaven, but I learned later that this was not true.

Sura IV Verse 124
If any do deeds

Of righteousness,
Be they male or female
And have faith,
They will enter Heaven,
And not the least in injustice
Will be done them.

However, the Prophet's descriptions of Heaven do seem to have men in mind. For what do most women care about the promise of chaste women in heaven for companions? (I wrote this a dozen years before the gay-lesbian-transgender movement took hold.)

Sura XXXVII Verse 48
And beside them will be
Chaste women; restraining
Their glances, with big eyes
(Of wonder and beauty).

Many men carried strings of prayer beads almost constantly. They appeared similar to the 'worry beads' that many European travelers associate with Greece. A Muslim man told me this about them;

> "During the Crusades and early Catholic Christian times, monks traveled through this country of Saudi Arabia and other Muslim countries with their rosaries. So the Muslims decided to copy this custom and made prayer beads with ninety-nine beads, one for each of the adjectives they use as names for Allah in the Koran: the Compassionate, the Kind, the Just, the All-Seeing, etc. etc. And the good Muslim then used the beads to say his prayers facing Mecca five times per day. But the ninety-nine bead string seemed too cumbersome a thing to carry, so they divided it into only thirty-three beads which is a much nicer size to carry. So now the good Muslim carries the beads and goes around three times saying the attributes of Allah and the one hundredth word is 'Allah!'"

Poor taxes were not well defined for me, though I did learn that one way of observing this injunction was to build a mosque in a poor section of the city where there was none and where none of the residents appeared able to afford to provide this integral community structure. Because I was with women who did not frequent mosques, their value as a center of community life did not come into focus for me until I attempted to respond to the invitation to visit the father of a friend to show him pictures of a site I had visited during a camping trip, a site where he had worked in years gone by. I arrived at exactly the time he had agreed to. He was not there. Where was he? He was at the mosque. But the last prayer time had been over for thirty minutes. "When will he be home"? I asked. The response was, "Oh, I don't know. He's probably busy talking with his friends there." I got the feeling that the mosque provided something more to Saudi men than our neighborhood bar provides for us; a community recreation center, religiously as well as figuratively. So providing a mosque as a '*zakat*' would be an important community service. Poor taxes are being redefined into an official taxation system. My understanding was that those businessmen with large enough incomes were summoned to the tax office to give an accounting and then told how much to contribute.

Fasting is the fourth pillar of Islam. Fortunately for me, I was in residence in the country during the first five days of Ramadan, which were my last five days in the Kingdom. I had heard reports from other expatriates, about the restrictions that had been imposed upon them, by their proximity to the fasting Muslims, but I had been saved from experiencing this until those last frantic days. In the hospital during Ramadan, the whole work schedule was adjusted so patients and staff could do as little work as possible during the fasting hours from dawn to sunset. Fasting during that period involved refraining from any drinks, water included, from food, from smoking and from sex. The hospital clinic and laboratory hours changed from the regular 8:30 am to 1 pm and 4:30 pm to 7:30 pm schedule to and 8 am to noon and a 9 pm to midnight schedule. Muslim patients and staff would not be asked to exert themselves during the fasting time. Non-Muslims who worked in offices were cautioned to bring all food and drinks with them to work and to lock their office doors when they partook so that they would not be seen to break the fast in front of their Muslim counterparts. In the few weeks before this fast, I could appreciably feel the tension rise as the Saudis anticipated this time of deprivation. Tempers became short. Police made more arrests. My Muslim colleagues appeared slightly frantic to make their exit from the country to less restrictive Muslim places.

I observed my students and female colleagues making up fasting days during the school year because they has had their menstrual period or been otherwise indisposed during the regular fasting time. The students would not make a big thing of it until near normal lunchtime when both mouth and stomach might begin to grumble.

When Ramadan started, just five days before I left the kingdom, I learned a little of what it felt like to be on a religious fast. The Saudi rules forbade all non-Muslims to eat, drink or smoke in front of fasting Muslims. We were cautioned that breaking that rule could cause our arrest. I was compelled during those 120'F to 130'F last days to rush from office to office in a frantic attempt to collect all monies due me from the University. I would drink as much water as my stomach would hold just before leaving the flat. Then I would walk the few blocks to the bus-stop; wait in the heat feeling my precious body fluids dripping down my sweaty arms. I tried to keep my mouth closed fearing to lose even more moisture that way. Finally, after five frustrating hours or rushing from office to office, I would again await the bus in the blazing heat, tasting in my mouth the change in my body chemistry caused by the loss of too much fluid.

Later, I lived in a home with a devout fasting Muslim woman and watched her experience the lethargy and nauseous feelings each evening as she forced herself to break her fast because she knew if she did not, she would not have the strength to endure the following day. One of my colleagues reported that outside Saudi Arabia, the danger of fasting was a frequent topic of discussion by health professionals.

The pilgrimage or haj is the fifth pillar of Islam. My knowledge of this most holy and inspiring event came from my Egyptian colleagues and Saudi students. We were given a two week holiday from classes. Both years, classes had not started on time, so classes were just postponed until after the holiday. Actually, because some students and teachers left a few days before the official holiday started, and some students were up to a week late returning, it meant we lost two teaching weeks out of the fifteen week semester. This sounds not too different from what goes on in our universities around Christmas holidays, except students in the USA are expected to be responsible for anything they missed. In Riyadh, the teachers were expected to be responsible that the students learn anything they missed.

The accounts given, upon their return sounded not very different from accounts any of us give after attending a seminar or retreat; that unexplainable feeling or wonder, of wholeness, of excitement of meeting people from afar who speak different languages and accents, yet share beliefs and that glorious uplifted feeling resulting from mass worship.

However, women did have special regulations and prohibitions. If she were menstruating or about to give birth, she was barred from participating with the masses. She had to perform a kind of pseudo pilgrimage in which she was forbidden to circumambulate or walk the seven times in the Holy Mosque. Menstruation or giving birth were considered to have defiled her and she had to be cleansed before participating. That made it difficult for women to perform that act which increased their chances of heaven. When one considered that the pilgrimage takes about ten days, of a month and women menstruate about six days, the chances of their being unable to complete the pilgrimage are considerable. Some of the women I knew got their doctors to prescribe hormones to delay menstruation so they could be 'clean' throughout the entire pilgrimage period.

In discussing it with me, one of my favorite students told me that a person is supposed to go at least once in a lifetime, if possible. If a woman has already gone once and her grandmother or mother never did, she can go again for that female relative. This adds blessings in heaven for her.

Another restriction for women was that they must not make the pilgrimage alone. A husband, father, son or brother must accompany her. To me the implication in this was that a woman could not meet her God alone. Why?

The outcome for me as a non-participant, was that the 'hajjis' or pilgrims almost always returned sick. Mingling with millions of people from over the globe who brought new microbes to which they were exposed by sleeping in dormitory tents, eating unaccustomed foods, using overcrowded restrooms and standing for long times together in the hot sun, and microbes to which they had not built up immunity, subjected their already stressed body systems to new disease invasions. Apparently one of the Prophet's traditions which included words from his own mouth about how to deal with pestilential outbreaks was;

"He who dies of epidemic disease is a martyr."

This implies immediate acceptance into heaven. My colleagues would be well into the infectious stage by the time they arrived on the first day back at work. Since teachers would be docked pay if they weren't there the first day after holidays, they came to class sick and shared their germs with all of us. About the second week of class, non-Muslim teachers would all be sick from whatever the *hajjis* brought back. This occurred during both years of my stay.

The pilgrimage, historically and commercially, is such an important part of Saudi life that they have one entire government ministry devoted to it. The feeling of responsibility for the millions, who poured through their shrines each year, had resulted in the formation of this government entity. Through this branch of officialdom were given out concessions for varying numbers of pilgrims. The concession holder was then able to take money from that many people and in exchange, provide for them the various necessities of the pilgrimage.

On my train trip down the Nile River in Egypt, I saw the quaint murals painted on houses of those who had completed the pilgrimage. Usually, the mural included an airplane, the airport in Jeddah which was the world's largest airport at that time, the special white ihram clothing and the Holy Mosque in Mecca.

Another way in which women were kept from the integral part of the religion was at funerals. Many of us will acknowledge how important our religion can become to us at the ritual observance of the various stages of life; birth, puberty, marriage and death. Muslim women did not attend funerals in the mosque or at the graveside. This came into my awareness when King Khalid died just fourteen days before my departure. I was so busy packing and preparing, I allowed myself only a few moments to watch the televised eulogy in the mosque at a friend's flat as my TV was already on its way home by ship. Suddenly it occurred to me that there were no women there or at the graveside which was shown a few moments later. I asked some of my Muslim colleagues about this. They reported that even in more liberal Muslim countries, women did not participate in public mourning. I confirmed this for myself later when I saw a funeral procession in Cairo. No women!

Because of the injunctions against any religious observances except Islam, the Christian community had to function literally 'underground'. No catacombs, just no visibility outside private Western compound walls. The American National Council of Churches sponsored a pastor there to minister to the Christian flocks. During the first year and one third of my stay, I attended services of that group though my own denominational affiliation is different. I felt the need for attending church and being with others from the Judeo-Christian heritage. The compound in which we met allowed the use of a large recreation room. Because the volume of worshippers, there were two English services and one in Arabic attended mostly by Egyptian Coptic Catholics. The Pakistanis held their Urdu services in one of the work camps outside the city. Altogether, there was a large a well organized and cohesive Christian community. Some of the extracurricular activities included adult and youth classes, religious education for children, group singing, a singles group, regular prayer groups, discussion groups, a drama group, desert outings and prison visits. The singles group always had a married couple as sponsor in order to comply with Saudi law that unmarried men and women should never be unchaperoned. I personally participated by teaching children, joining the drama group, attending singles parties and desert outings.

A short while into my second year, the Christian group was asked to stop meeting in the big company compound. Some people suspected that the Saudi government had become alarmed by the Bahrain incident in which a group of Iranian revolutionaries had used Bahrain as a site to foment plots. Any assembly of people had become suspect. The Christian Fellowship broke into smaller groups and met in individuals villas. The Christian community responded to this fragmentation with a truly inspiring energy. Almost all the former activities were quickly resumed within the altered context. Regardless of the expatriate's feelings about 'organized religion', most agreed that this group provided a service to the whole Western community. It was a service in providing connections with our own cultural roots, which the Saudis forbade to be publicly observed.

The repression of 'unacceptable' religious observances occasionally took bizarre forms. On December 24, 1981, I made the following entry in my journal;

"This morning, we had our second annual Christmas party for the patients on the spinal cord injury unit. Last year before I was involved with this unit, they gave the patients a Christmas party and the director of the hospital was so pleased because he said it was the first party that had even been given for the patients by the staff in any of the Kingdom's Ministry of Health hospitals. He praised the staff. So a party was planned again for this season. And permission given.

We decorated the physical therapy gym. The nurses made a crepe-paper Christmas tree and decorated it with their own Christmas cards from the Philippines. The Filipina nurses and the Korean physiotherapists made wonderful food. We practiced Jingle Bells and Deck the Halls, both secular songs.

This morning, I put on my long red jumper made newly for this season, put tinsel in my hair and got a ride with a friend for me, my autoharp, incense, more tinsel and my Christmas cassette tapes. At the hospital, as with all parties, it was supposed to start at 10:00 am but of course people didn't start to arrive until after 10:45 am. The head nurse wished everybody a Merry Christmas. Then we served the patients. Our guests, the doctors, nurses, social workers from other units served themselves. Lastly, our staff ate. Such good stuff! Homemade doughnuts, batter fried shredded vegetables with grated ginger in it, roasted chicken, special spiced Filipino sausages, chicken sandwiches, cake, etc. Delicious stuff!

We were told we couldn't sing our songs. We had planned to do it just before eating but the Matron or Director of Nurses as she would be know in the USA came just before we were to do it and said, "Don't sing! Wait until all the guests are gone." Well about 11:25 am she came and said, "Please take down the Christmas cards in the halls" She had one in her hands that evidently someone outside, maybe a mutawah, had ripped off the wall. It was a photo of a Filipino beach with folks in swimming, running on the beach. Well these rigid Wahabis don't like idols and photos were idols to them, especially in swim suits. The people in that photo were so small; you had to really squint to see that they were in swim suits. Anyway, we quickly took down all the decorations in the hall. We began to clean up the gym. Two Koreans had put on their beautiful national dresses and were singing a song for the patients, when the head nurse said to me that she and I had to go down to the director's office and, "STOP THE KOREANS FROM SINGING!" So we went down. Also the Matron, the Korean hostel matron, the Filipino hostel matron all joined us in the director's office. The acting director, who was taking the place of the director who was in the USA for medical treatment, gave us a little lecture on how embarrassed he was because somebody had complained about this Christian celebration. He was sure it was a misunderstanding but please take down all the decorations in the hospital. He didn't want the hospital's reputation impugned. He had not anticipated this trouble when he had given his permission a few weeks previously. But we must all be aware that public practice of any religion but Islam was forbidden so please 'cool it'. And thanks for coming.

So I went upstairs and told the Korean physiotherapists to please take down ALL the decorations. Fortunately, the real party was over before this brouhaha occurred. The patients were all wishing us Merry Christmas. What an experience! Actually, it was quite interesting. For only two minutes did I fear jail or deportation."

My first year, I was unprepared for 'Christmas harassment.' Our college had been promising to move the Department of Nursing from the villa to the main women's campus for months, when in the week before Christmas which fell on Thursday, the weekend, we were told we would have to move on December 25th. Of course, when we pointed out that it was our major religious holiday, the administration said "Just pack up and mark everything before". This sort of thing was so subtle that a firm accusation of harassment could not be attached to it, except that the accumulation of such occurrences made us feel 'persecuted'. In a letter to my sister I referred to such situations in the following paragraph;

"As recently as 1949, these Arabs were willing to just kill a Christian or any other non-Believer for just crossing their borders. They wouldn't give a foreigner a visa and if they caught him, they killed him according to Wilfred Thesiger (1980) Sometimes now, Americans and British get very cross with them for not giving visas to families and travelers fast enough, but it was only 30 years ago, they weren't giving visas. So actually, it is something of an improvement. Frequently, Westerners think they are just being 'hassled' by the Arabs. But I believe it is more just a long habit, part of their modus operandi to delay and be indecisive."

Much of what happened to me, what I saw could not be judged by previous standards of my culture. My impact on them, I am sure was non-existent. But their impact on me? I will forever see the world differently than I did before. The struggle to achieve women's rights has a different meaning to me after living their way.

REFERENCES:

Al-Asqalani, Ibn Hajar (1428) *The Hadith*. Publisher unknown.

Al Omar, Professor Abdul Rahman Ben Hammad (1975) *Islam: the Religion of Truth*. Riyadh: Supreme Head Office for Religious Researches, Ifta, Call and Guidance Departments.

Ali, Abdallah Yousef (1931) *The Quran*, Egypt.

Thesiger, Wilfred (1980) *The Last Nomad*. New York: E. P. Dutton.

15

EPILOGUE

The rights of Saudi women have made little progress since I left the Kingdom in 1982. Reports from both the United Nation Committee on Elimination of Discrimination against Women and also Human Rights Watch (2008) have made recent reviews on this issue and both agree, that there is little attention paid in Saudi Arabia to the 1979 international Bill of Rights for Women. Women still need permission of a close male relative to see a doctor, to seek employment, to apply for travel documents or tickets. Even foreign women such as 24-year-old Nazia Quazi who holds both an Indian and a Canadian citizenship is a victims of Saudi disregard of international laws. She is essentially held prisoner in Saudi Arabia by her Indian father who confiscated both her Indian and Canadian passports thus depriving her of the capability to get an exit visa (Pollitt 2010).

Historically, it has been common for older men to marry child brides. This practice is coming under government regulation at last. This trend has come about because of a situation in which an eight year old girl was married to a sixty year old man. The mother wanted the marriage annulled but the father who had gotten dowry money for the child bride did not agree. The girl plans to ask for a divorce as soon as she is old enough to be recognized by the government (*BBC News* 2009). In another case, an eight-year-old who had been forced into marriage by her father was allowed to divorce the fifty-year-old man. A Saudi human rights activist is hoping to get a law passed to make eighteen be the minimum age for females to marry (Al-Shalchi 2009)

Women also suffer from high rates of illiteracy and domestic violence. The United Nations report also addresses the plight of female foreign domestic

140

workers such as the young woman to whom I talked in prison. Little has changed since 1982 as the Saudi government continued to deny that women are discriminated against. As late as 2009 the Saudi judicial system permitted men to slap their wives (Shihri 2009). However, some small steps are being taken; women were allowed to work in mixed-sex shopping areas which previously had been *harram* or forbidden. In 2006, the National Society of Human Rights opened a domestic violence shelter. Bans on both books and movies which had previously been forbidden have been lifted (Akbar 2006). A hotel for "women only" opened in early 2008. It is owned and run by women for women. Some protest that it furthers the existing segregation of the sexes. But since much of a regular hotel is forbidden to women, such as the health spa and main dining rooms, many business women who have used it, praise the freedom they feel there. The following was reported in the August 7, 2008 *Women's E-News*

> "Saudi officials and anti-violence advocates met in Jeddah on July 15 to discuss improving coordination between agencies, the Khaleej Times reported. Goals laid out in the meeting include ensuring that all victims are provided shelter and legal assistance and penalties are increased for abusers".

Women are fighting back. Men from the Commission for the Propagation of Virtue and the Prevention of Vice who walk the streets to discipline women who are not well enough covered were sprayed with pepper spray by two women who called the men "terrorists". They were released after apologizing. (*The Week* 2007). None-the-less, this was a risky act for them as are attempts at free speech. A Saudi blogger was arrested in December 2007. He had written about political prisoners (Zoepf 2008). However, a more recent article from *The Economist* speculates that these segregated sex rules may be loosening due to more liberal thought from the Saudi jurisprudence (*The Economist*, 1-7-2010).

At a conference on "Gender Research in the Arab Region" held in Beirut mentions no Saudi Women among the 30 delegates. However, one important issue was presented by Iman Azzi (2008), the Arabic language had no word for 'gender'. This is simply transliterated from the English. Absence of a word often means the concept is not considered in writings or conversation, thus making a concept hard for people to grasp. Both of these facts reinforce the assertions of the United Nations and Human Rights Watch that women's issues receive short shrift in Saudi Arabia. However, in a more positive direction, a female minister was appointed as a deputy education minister for a new department for women's education (Borger 2009). Previously there had been no female at that level in the Saudi government.

When I went to Saudi Arabia in 1980, though I had read four books on the country before arriving there, including the US State Department book, I understood very little about the schism between the Sunnis and the Shiites. I understood even less about how this divide was the cause of the increasing repression of all residents of the country, particularly women. I had heard that the royal family feared a takeover by the religious leader like that of Iran the year before I arrived. I was unaware of the implications of the Shia leadership in the revolution of Iran. The stability by the two sects which Iraq maintained for so many years was significantly disturbed in Saudi Arabia according to Megan Stack (2006). The fact that the Shia in Iraq were able to get out from under Saddam Hussein's Sunni rule has inspired Saudi Shia to envision the same for themselves. This situation keeps the Saudi ruling family constantly on edge and maintaining all the repressions of the last decades.

There is a world-wide effort among some Muslim women scholars to take a new look and possibly different interpretation of the Koran. In New York City in 2006 women from twenty five countries began to organize to examine the Islamic religious texts from a female perspective of the law. The issues that most concern these women are inheritance, domestic violence, and divorce. In several Muslim countries women have been named by their government or community as '*muftias*', women who can issue *fatwa*'s which is a scholarly opinion of a moral or religious dilemma (Arnoldy 2006). *Mufti* has all been made up of males up until a few years ago. This is a hopeful sign though Saudi women apparently did not attend the organizational meeting.

Women are discussing the pros and cons of Ramadan fasting in a way not previously known. Islam puts a priority on the child's health rather than the mother's desires. So breast feeding women are discouraged from fasting during Ramadan. Some recent studies show definite hazards for pregnant women. They are prone to have cesareans, to need induced labor and for the infant to need special care. Fetal breathing decreases during fasting. Women's breast milk is less nutritious due to vitamin deficiencies when all the eating is crammed into a few hours rather than spaced over the day. Both infant and mother are liable to suffer dehydration. Gestational diabetes is a greater risk for fasting mothers. As stated earlier in the book, women who do not fast due to menstruation, pregnancy or breast feeding must make up missed fasting days before the next Ramadan season. While it is the author's opinion that fasting in the desert is almost always unhealthy, it is particularly hard for women due to the issues presented by Soquel (2007).

Shankar Vedantam (2008) quotes Michael Ross at the University of California at Los Angeles; "Oil wealth, not Islam, is the primary reason that these nations have regressive gender policies." Women usually do the manufacturing jobs in a culture until the sorts of construction jobs required as in the oil industry begin to predominate. Women then stay home and have their access to political knowledge curtailed. As oil profits soar, women stay home and their power decreases. However, in Saudi Arabia, with urbanization, women have left the task of herding animals and collecting camel chips for fuel. While Ross's theory may indeed apply, Saudi women have had little part in the economy of the country except as child-bearers since expatriate servants are almost universally employed in Saudi homes for the past decades.

In 1982, some of my female Saudi students confessed to having driven cars out in the desert where there were no police. But the struggle to legalize driving for women has continued. In 2007 a group of women petitioned the King for the right to drive. They fell back on economic reasons rather than a human rights or equality rationale. It is too expensive to hire a driver they said. When about fifty women staged a driving protest in 1990, they went to jail, lost their passports and jobs. This time, electronics has assisted the women. Their petition to the King was circulated on e-mail (Abu-Nasr 2007). The male professor who encouraged his wife and the other women was arrested (Ambah 2008c). One of the continuing problems for women has been that they required a male's permission for almost any public transaction, which makes it difficult to stage a revolution. But electronic communication has bitten into this part of Saudi male control as so many opportunities are offered to communicate unsupervised via the Internet.

Several popular TV shows have dealt with the issue of women driving (Abou-Alsamh 2007). The Saudi National Human Rights Association is doing research on this issue. I was surprised to learn of the existence of this association as there was certainly no evidence of such a movement when I was living there. Newspapers have begun to have articles on this subject. Corruption of the family will follow assert the religious conservatives and their imams. The message they send that women cannot control their baser desires still flourishes in that regressive group. More women work all the time and need more flexible transportation than relying on the family driver. This is another way the Internet has influenced women because they have seen women diving in other countries and envied this freedom. The organization League of Demanders of Women's Rights to Drive Cars in Saudi Arabia is quite a surprising development. One of the co-founders Wajeha al-Huwaider says "Cats and dogs in the developed world have more rights than Arab women." (*Women's E-News* 2007). During the flood of Jeddah in November 2009, a teenage girl ferried nine van loads of stranded people to safety without repercussions of the Committee for the Promotion of Virtue and the Prevention of Vice (*The Economist* 2010).

Some prophesied that women would be allowed to drive by the end of the year 2008 through a royal decree. Saudi women have had one recent victory in that they are now allowed to register singly at a hotel if they provide proper identifying documents, however, the police will be given their identity information. The originators of the current movement for women to be allowed to drive acknowledge that it will be chaos at the beginning but that soon women driving will be perfectly acceptable (Ambah 2008a).

In Chapter 8, I refer to the 1981 *The World Press* Review article called "Saudi Arabia's Race with Time". The writer wrote about "A class of pampered Saudis and a sub-class of insecure foreign helots." This situation has not much changed as author Rasheed Abou-Alsamh (2007) describes the current generation in Saudi Arabia 'spoiled rotten'. He goes on to chastise his fellow citizens for being arrogant and lazy. The question he does not ask is what will happen when foreigners are no longer there to do all the mundane task that make modern living possible. Will they have forgotten how to care for themselves?

Islamic law has seemed to disregard women practitioners because few women were allowed in positions of leadership in any profession. However, *Women's E-News* (2007) reports that they are now able to study law at King Abdul Aziz University. Who can tell what that will mean to the harsh treatments Muslim women have suffered through the ages for sexual transgressions? In 2007, a 19 year old woman in Qatif on the shores of the Persian Gulf was out with an unrelated man. The young man was her former boyfriend and they were meeting so he could return some photos since she was going to marry someone else. They were sitting in a parked car. They were both raped by their attackers. Each was sentenced to 90 lashes because they had been out unchaperoned together. Their attackers were given a number of different sentences of jail-time and lashes. The man appealed the attackers' sentences saying they were not harsh enough. The Islamic judge increased the female victim's sentence to 200 lashes (Abou-Alsamh 2007c). There was such an outcry from Saudi women as well as from the international community, that the King pardoned the female rape victim of the punishment of lashes (Agence France-Presse 2007; Ambah 2007; BBC News 2007) .

The situation has not improved for foreign women workers in Saudi Arabia, workers such as the young Sri Lankan woman I described visiting in jail in Chapter 12 on Justice. In 2007 another nineteen year old Sri Lankan domestic worker was bottle feeding a four month old infant when it choked and died. She was given the death sentence though her confession was a paper in Arabic which she was not able to read; nor was she given a lawyer. She was seventeen years old at the time. Through the support of Human Rights Watch, Amnesty International and Hong Kong-based Asian-Human Rights

Commission, she appealed her conviction (Habib 2007). Her case is apparently still unresolved as I was unable to find the outcome through Google. Several European governments petitioned the king on her behalf. According to Habib (2007), the Sri Lankan embassy reports that one hundred fifty females flee their Saudi employers each month. They like I was, are required to relinquish their passports to their employers. They are overworked, sexually harassed by employers unlike me. They are often cheated out of their wages just as I was, though their wages are minuscule compared to mine and their families are dependent on their earnings. King Abdullah Ben Abdelaziz Al Saud surprised the world when he went to call at the Vatican Wednesday July 16, 2008. Apparently part of his goal was to smooth out hostility over the way in which many Catholic Filipinos and Filipinas are treated by their employers (*Le Monde* 2008). I wonder how this will help these workers. Will this make the judicial *imams* deal with them more kindly? This visit to the Vatican was part of his attendance and sponsorship of the World Conference on Dialogue in Madrid, Spain. Apparently he had convened a similar conference six weeks before in Saudi Arabia for Islamic scholars and intellectuals (Lerner 2008).

One of the most amusing recent occurrences was when the Commission for the Propagation of Virtue and the Prevention of Vice banned men from publicly walking pets. This was to prevent men from luring women while walking dogs or cats (Abu-Nasr 2008).

In a world in which sports is a main way for cultures to meet, the development of Saudi women's basketball teams is definitely progress even though they are not yet allowed to leave the country to compete. Jeddah, the western coastal city has been more liberal in many arenas and that is where the "Jiddah United" women's basketball team plays outside in the heat wearing sweat pants and jerseys. Public school sports are banned for girls but these athletes are women. In 1990 all gyms for women were closed. Those associated with hospitals have recently been reopened (Ambah 2008b). In 2009, the Saudi government is closing all women's gyms again because there is no overseeing body to register female gyms. Men's' gyms are over seen by the government (*Women's E-News* 2009). Small steps! Pressures from the European countries and the US and Canada have mixed results. Sometimes the King responds to appeals from Western powers but many times, the conservative religious men maintain their hold on the culture and their oppression of women.

REFERENCES:

Abou-Alsamh, Rasheed (2007a) Saudis Rethink Taboo on Women behind the Wheel, *New York Times*, 9-28-07.

Abou-Alsamh, Rasheed (2007b) Unable to Live without Our Servants, *The Week,* 8-31-07.

Abou-Alasmh, Rasheed (2007c) Ruling Jolts Even Saudis: 200 Lashes for Rape. *The New York Times,* 11-6-07.

Abu-Nasr, Donna (2007) Saudi Women Lobby King for Driving Right. *The Associated Press,* Monday, 9-17-07.

Abu-Nasr, Donna (2008) Dogs, cats banned in effort to part sexes: City aims to keep men from making passes at women. Associated Press in the *Hilo Herald-Tribune,* 8-1-08.

Agence France-Presse (2007) Saudi Women Activists Furious at Gang-Rape Ruling *Agence France-Presse,* 11-22-07.

Akbar, Arifa (2006) Hello Boys: Lingerie Leads the Fight for Saudi Women's Rights, *The Independent UK,* 4-27-06.

Al-Shalchi, Hadeel (2009) 8-year-old Saudi divorces 50-year-old husband. *Associated Press* 5-1-09.

Ambah, Faiza Saleh (2007) Rights Advocate Fights Back, *Washington Post Foreign Service,* 11-29-07.

Ambah, Faiza Saleh (2008a) Saudi Women See a Brighter Road on Rights, *Washington Pos Foreign Service,* 1-31-08.

Ambah, Faiza Saleh (2008b) A Drive toward the Goal of Greater Freedom, *Washington Post Foreign Service,* 4-15-08.

Ambah, Faiza Saleh (2008c) *Washington Post Foreign Service,* Wednesday, 5-21-08; p. A13.

Arnoldy, Ben (2006) Bid to Bring Female Voice to Islamic Law, *Christian. Science Monitor,* 11-21-06

Azzi, Iman (2008) Arab World Forum Shares Gender Field Notes 1-18-08 *Women's E-news.*

BBC News (2007) Saudi King 'pardons rape victim' *BBC News,* 12-17-07.

BBC News (2009) Saudis 'to regulate' child brides. *BBC News,* 4-15-09.

Bhatia, Julie (2009) Cheers and Jeers. *Women's E-News, 5-8-09*

Borger, Julian (2009) Saudi Arabia Appoints First Female Minister. *The Guardian,* 2-16-09.

Habib, Shahnaz (2007) Death Sentence Looms over Sri Lankan Teen Migrant, *Women's E-News,* 12-21-07.

Human Rights Watch Report (2008) *Women's E-News,* 5-2-08

Le Monde (2008) Saudi Overview. *Le Monde Editorial,* 7-18-08.

Learner, Michael (2008) My Talk with the Saudis, and What I learned from Them. *Tikkun,* 7-20-08.

Murphy, Caryle (2008) Saudi Arabia's First Women-Only Hotel: Is it Progress? *The Christian Science Monitor.* 5-13-08.

Pollitt, Katha (2010) Free Nazia Quazi. *The Nation* p. 8. 2-8-10.

Shihri, Abdullah (2009) Saudi Judge Says it's OK for Men to Beat Wives. *The Associated Press,* 5-13-09.

Soquel, Dominique (2007) Ramadan Feeds Mixed Views on Maternal Fasts *Women's E-News,* 10-2-07.

Stack, Megan (2006) Iraqi Strife Seeping into Saudi Kingdom, *Los Angeles Times,* 4-27-06

The Economist (2010) Not So Terrible After All? *The Economist.* 1-7-10.

The Week (2007) The World at a Glance. *The Week,* 10-5-07.

U.N. Committee on the Elimination of Discrimination against Women (2008) *Saudi restrictions on women questioned; a U.N. Panel takes the kingdom to task for curbing their rights.* Reuters. 1-18-08

United Nations Committee on Elimination of Discrimination (2008) *Saudi women face systematic discrimination: UN report.* 2-4-08

Vedantam, Shankar (2008) Petroleum Feeds Patriarch, *The Washington Post,* 3-10-08.

Women's E-News (2007) Saudi Women Studying Law, *Women's E-News,* 8-29-07.

Women's E-News (2007) Cheers, *Women's E-News* 10-1-07

Women's E-News (2008) Cheers and Jeers, *Women's E-News,* 8- 7-08.

Zoepf, Katherine (2008) Saudis Confirm Detention of Blogger, *The New York Times,* 1-2-08.

GLOSSARY OF ARABIC WORDS

Abaya – black cloak
Bedouin – nomad, more properly pronounced 'Bedu'
Belote – game played with small stones on the ground
Benzene – gasoline
Dala – Arabic coffee pot
En Sha Allah – If God wills it.
Fatwa – a religious opinion regarding Islamic law
Ghutra – men's head cloth
Haj – pilgrimage to the Holy Places of Islam
Hajjis – persons who have completed a pilgrimage
Halas - finished, complete
Hammam – toilet in the floor, originally meant 'bath'
Harram - forbidden
Harem – women's
Henna – herbal hair or skin dye
Hijera – migration or fleeing away from a place
Hommos – a paste made of ground seasoned chickpeas or garbanzos
Igal - black rings worn on men's head cloth
Igama – work permit or work visa
Ihram – special costume for making the pilgrimage
Imam – religious teacher
Islam – the religion started by the Prophet Mohammad
Jebel – mountain
Koran – the sacred writings revealed to Mohammad the Prophet
La – No

Maharram – males with whom it is alright for a woman to be alone, men she cannot marry or remarry; father, uncle, brother, son and husband.

Ma Salama – Be Safe! Or colloquially used for good-bye

Miqqua – dressing stations on the pilgrimage road

Mosque – house of worship in Islam

Mufti – people who can make fatwas.

Mutawah – religious policeman

Qur'an or *Quran* – the sacred writings revealed to Mohammad the Prophet

Rababa – one stringed instrument

Ramadan – the month for fasting

Riyadh - garden, also the capital of Saudi Arabia

Riyal – unit of money worth approximately 34 cents in 1980

Sedik – friend

Sediki - the Westerners' name for grain alcohol

Shariah or *Shari'ah* – religious law of Islam

Sheik – old man, teacher, or rich man

Sohbah – safe company

Souq – market place

Thobe – men's robe

Umra – lesser pilgrimage

Ude – mandolin like musical instrument

Wadi – ravine or wash

Wahabi – literally Unitarian, or colloquially the puritanical sect of Islam

Zakat - the poor tax or alms required of Muslims